Learning from Errors in Rational Emotive Behaviour Therapy

Learning from Errors in Rational Emotive Behaviour Therapy

by
MICHAEL NEENAN
Centre for Stress Management, London

AND

WINDY DRYDEN
Goldsmiths College, University of London

W

WHURR PUBLISHERS
LONDON AND PHILADELPHIA

© 2001 Whurr Publishers

First published 2001 by
Whurr Publishers Ltd
19b Compton Terrace, London N1 2UN, England
325 Chestnut Street, Philadelphia PA19106, USA

British Library Cataloguing in Publication Data

A catalogue record for this book is available from the British Library.

ISBN 1 86156 301 9

Printed and bound in the UK by Athenaeum Press Limited, Gateshead, Tyne & Wear.

Contents

Part II: Assessment Errors

Part III: Goal-Setting Errors

Part IV: Disputing Errors

Part V: Homework Errors

Part VI: Working-Through Errors

Part VII: Self-Maintenance Errors

Preface

In our considerable experience of teaching REBT, we have noticed a large number of common errors that students regularly make (in fact, we can reliably predict what most of these errors will be). One weekend, we got together to note down all the common errors we could think of as the basis for a future book. Initially, we aimed for fifty or sixty, thinking this would be the limit, but once we got started we had trouble stopping; we finally ran out of steam at one hundred and one. We decided to assemble all the errors into seven categories: general, assessment, goal setting, disputing, homework, working through and self-maintenance. With each error, we have explained what has gone wrong and how to put it right. The dialogue excerpts in each error are not verbatim accounts of therapy or supervision but illustrative examples of the points we are making.

We hope that students reading this book will be able to pinpoint these errors at an earlier stage in their training, thereby helping them to make faster progress towards becoming competent REBT therapists. Finally, we do not intend in any way to 'poke fun' at our students for making these errors but simply to state the obvious: errors are an inextricable part of learning anything new. So, in the spirit of learning from our mistakes, we dedicate this book to our students.

Michael Neenan
Windy Dryden
London
March 2001

PART I:
GENERAL ERRORS

1 Exploring for too long clients' expectations of REBT and their previous experiences of therapy

While these are important issues to explore, trainees frequently let this exploration cover the whole first session thereby holding up problem assessment (which should ideally start in the first session). Once clients' expectations of therapy have been confirmed, modified or disconfirmed by you and previous experiences of therapy have been divided into helpful and unhelpful elements, then ask for a problem. However, in this extract, the trainee seeks to understand the client's difficulties with previous therapy:

Client: I didn't like the therapy I had before because the therapist didn't say very much. I felt very uncomfortable with all the silences.

Trainee: I wonder why you are uncomfortable with silences?

[Instead of asking a highly predictable question, the trainee could have told the client about the lack of silence in REBT sessions and wondered whether she would be comfortable with such a high level of verbal activity.]

Client: I just feel awkward with them. If I ask a question, then I would like a reply. At times, it was like getting blood out of a stone.

Trainee: Why is getting a reply so important to you?

[The trainee could have told her that she will get replies to her questions in REBT – which she will find out about in a few minutes. Unfortunately, REBT gets postponed until the next session as the trainee pursues his own idiosyncratic agenda.]

Whatever issues have not been covered in an initial exploration of clients' expectations and previous experiences of therapy can be dealt with by you, if and when they emerge, while you are conducting REBT (e.g. 'I thought you would be focusing on my childhood, not the present', 'I didn't do homework in my previous therapy; so why do I have to do it now?').

Key Point

Information regarding these issues should not detain you for long. Problem assessment is your prime concern in the first session.

2 Developing the therapeutic relationship first

The therapeutic relationship has a hallowed place in psychotherapy; it has to be established before any other interventions can proceed. The 'sacredness' of this relationship means you will often spend a lot of time nurturing it by, among other things, showing respect, establishing trust, demonstrating empathy and offering unconditional positive regard (or, in REBT terms, unconditional acceptance). Only when the relationship has been developed through this process can a problem assessment begin. Grieger and Boyd (1980) call this the 'myth of the relationship' and state that the relationship has no independent function or existence: its usefulness stems from the likelihood that it promotes client change rather than hinders it. A productive relationship can be developed through an early problem-solving focus:

Trainee: Surely you have to show the client you care before asking for a problem, otherwise it all seems so impersonal?

Supervisor: Asking for a problem, understanding it accurately from the client's viewpoint and then showing the client how to ameliorate it, isn't that a powerful way of showing that you care?

Trainee: I suppose so, but how can the client reveal his innermost secrets to you, if you haven't developed trust?

Supervisor: How can you be sure he will eventually reveal his innermost secrets to you? It's better to start working on a problem rather than waiting for the core problem to emerge and then the client can see your problem-solving skills in action. If he thinks you are competent, then he is more likely to reveal his innermost secrets.

Trainee: Okay, good point. One last thing then: isn't REBT going against the grain in not seeing the relationship as important?

Supervisor: It's important but not all-important, we don't worship at its shrine. Problems are solved by doing something constructive about them rather than spending an inordinate amount of time on the nuts and bolts of building a relationship. Some clients will leave therapy early because you are not getting down to the business of helping them, while others may become increasingly dependent on the relationship instead of them becoming increasingly competent problem solvers.

Developing and maintaining a relationship needs some attention from you but your primary focus is on helping your client to become his own therapist.

Key Point

Remember that developing a therapeutic relationship and initiating an early problem-solving focus are concurrent activities in REBT.

3   Not setting or keeping to a therapeutic agenda

Agenda setting helps to keep both you and your client focused on the respective tasks that need to be undertaken in order to make the optimum use of therapy time. Agenda setting also emphasizes the structured approach of REBT, but you may feel that structure is synonymous with straitjacket and therefore dispense with it:

Trainee: This is your time and space; so what would you like to talk about?

[This question acts as a possible invitation to let therapy wander instead of providing structure to the session.]

Client: Well, a lot has been happening in the last week. The weather for one thing – it's been dreadful. My brother's having more trouble with his wife, they're always arguing those two. The television's on the blink again. If it isn't one thing, then it's another.

This structureless approach can lead to chitchat, endless pleasantries, meandering conversations, jumping from one topic to another with both parties eventually wondering where therapy is going. Agenda setting is part of the process of socializing your clients into REBT so that they realize what will be expected of them in each session:

Therapist: As usual, let's start with the agenda. I'd like to review your homework, come back to your guilt feelings we discussed last week, negotiate further homework, and get end-of-session feedback. What items would you like to put on the agenda?

Client: Well, I didn't do the homework because my husband was in a foul mood because of what's happening at work and –

Therapist: May I stop you there? It's important to put the items on the agenda before discussing them.

[You may have experienced this problem frequently, but it is important to interrupt to teach your client what agenda setting means.]

Client: Oh, all right. I'd like to discuss my brother because he's having real problems with his wife.

Therapist: Are you particularly upset about your brother's difficulties with his wife?

[The therapist is seeking the relevance of this problem for discussion. If the client is upset, then this would become an agenda item.]

Client: No, but I thought you could give me some advice to pass on to him.

Therapist: The items on the agenda are about your problems, not other people's. So, with you as the focus, what shall I put down?

Client: Well, I wonder whether I can really change at my age. Can you really help me?

[Therapist writes this down.]

Therapist: Anything else?

Client: Not for the present.

Therapist: Okay. Now what prevented you from carrying out the agreed homework?

Proficient agenda setting takes no more than a couple of minutes, so aim for this time target, but, as Walen et al. point out: 'Agenda setting is a skill that requires training, supervision and lots and lots of practice' (1992: 66). Agenda setting is a flexible procedure; so if your client comes to the session feeling suicidal or bursts into tears in the session, then this becomes the agenda for immediate discussion. As well as not setting an agenda, you may also have trouble keeping to it once it is set:

Supervisor: (listening to a session tape) You're both discussing *Eastenders*. Was this an agreed agenda item?

Trainee: No, but the client said how much she liked it, and I do too, and we sort of got talking about it.

Supervisor: Did the discussion have any clinical relevance?

Trainee: No, but it might help strengthen the therapeutic bond, that sort of thing.

Supervisor: That could also be strengthened through pursuing problem-solving strategies. What message might you be sending about the agenda?

Trainee: I'm not sure.

Supervisor: If you stress the importance of setting the agenda at the beginning of every session, then it is equally important to . . . what?

Trainee: Keep to it. I suppose I do let therapy wander into these areas of non-clinical interest. Thinking about it now, I wander from the agenda quite often.

Supervisor: What might be an in-session task for you then?

Trainee: Monitor how often I drift from the agenda and note the reasons for it.

Supervisor: (with emphasis) And tackle those reasons!

Key Point

Set an agenda in every session and then keep to it in every session.

4 Not being active and directive

REBT therapists usually adopt an active-directive style. They are active in, among other things, asking questions, collecting assessment data, limiting client rambling or generalities, formulating hypotheses, problem defining, goal setting, disputing irrational beliefs and negotiating homework tasks. Through these and other activities, they direct their clients to the cognitive core (i.e. irrational beliefs) of their emotional and behavioural problems. REBT deems this approach to be more effective in helping clients change than a passive or non-directive style of intervention. I (WD) have stated that, in over twenty years as a trainer of REBT therapists, being active-directive is the 'aspect of the therapy with which most trainees struggle. This is especially the case with trainees who have had prior training in person-centred therapy or psychodynamic therapy' (1995: 22). If clients are to learn REBT, then they follow your lead rather than you follow theirs. In this example, the trainee is following the client:

Client: Everything is falling apart. I don't know what to do. Maybe no one can help me. The stress I'm under is unbelievable.

Trainee: Things sound pretty horrible for you at the moment.

[The trainee's question is an encouragement for the client to keep talking in general terms about his problems. You can be both empathic and problem focused in your response; so the trainee could have added: 'Can you give me a current or recent example of "everything is falling apart"?']

Client: I've got everyone at me over this business, the work is piling up, I can't meet the deadlines, my wife is threatening to leave me.

Trainee: I wonder how you're feeling about all this?

[Possible approaches could have been to clarify what 'this business' means or ask the client which of the three problem areas he has revealed he would like to start working on.]

Client: I'm so angry it's affecting my sleep, I can't think straight and I snap at everyone. I'm sure my blood pressure is going through the roof.

Trainee: So you're angry, and it's obviously having a bad effect on your life. In what other ways is your anger having an unhelpful effect on your life?

['What are you specifically angry about?' or 'What thoughts make you angry and in what situations?' could start to orientate the client to the type of information required for a problem analysis. The trainee keeps the focus on the consequences of the client's anger instead of directing his attention to his anger-producing thinking.]

In our experience, most clients have no difficulties in accepting an active-directive approach once you explain the rationale for it. Clients expect some problem-solving action from you and being active-directive can usually help to bring this about in a relatively brief period of time. In order to increase your own level of active-directiveness, review your session audiotapes, engage in role plays with other trainees, watch videos of leading REBT therapists in action and read transcripts of their therapy sessions. In the following extract, the therapist focuses the client's attention very quickly on her guilt-inducing thinking:

Client: I feel very guilty about what I did.

Therapist: What exactly did you do that you feel guilty about?

[The therapist's question wants to root the guilt in a specific context.]

Client: I slept with my husband's best friend. My husband has always been faithful to me. That's why I feel guilty.

Therapist: Not everyone would feel guilty about sleeping with someone else, whether or not their partner is faithful; so it is important to discover what thoughts go through your mind that lead you to feel guilty about what you did.

[The therapist teaches the client the importance of the thought–feeling link in producing her guilt.]

Client: I shouldn't have done it. Why did I do it?

Therapist: But as you did do it . . . ?

[The therapist keeps the client focused on what she did rather than allow her at this point to explore the reasons for her behaviour. This procedure elicits her self-appraisal.]

Client: I see myself as a devious person for what I did. In fact, a slut.

Therapist: Your guilt appears to have two components: one, you did something you should not have done and, two, because of your action you condemn yourself as a 'devious person, a slut'. Is that correct?

[The therapist summarizes the information presented in order to check whether the cognitive components of the client's guilt have been established.]

Client: (nodding) That's it.

Being active-directive keeps clients on track as you guide them through the ABCDE model of self-disturbance and change.

Key Point

Learn to be active-directive so you can keep your clients on track in therapy.

---

5   Not wanting to intervene in the client's problem without knowing the 'big picture' first

This error is called 'the big-picture trap' because you 'insist on obtaining a total picture of the client's past, present and future before beginning an intervention program' (Grieger and Boyd, 1980: 77). You may see this as a safety procedure instead of a trap because you believe that, when you are armed with all the facts, you will better understand the client's problem and thereby tackle it more effectively. We consider this viewpoint a poor use of therapy time and REBT:

Supervisor: (listening to the session tape) The client said he felt anxious around people who are better educated than he is. Why did you not ask him 'What are you most anxious about' rather than explore his educational history?

Trainee: Well, I thought exploring his educational history would offer some clues to his anxiety.

Supervisor: But you could have found that out immediately and directly by asking him the question I suggested.

Trainee: Okay, but I found out that he didn't go to university; so that could be a reason for his anxiety around better-educated people.

Supervisor: It's his appraisal of not going to university that you want to discover, not simply the fact he didn't go. Again, you could have simply asked him. The client's present problems are filtered through the ABC model, and the B is the crucial part to locate. Collecting a mass of information just delays this process.

Trainee: But isn't the big picture important?

Supervisor: You can piece together the big picture as more information emerges, while you are undertaking a problem assessment in REBT terms.

It is not necessary to get the big picture before you start therapy or even after it has started.

If you educate yourself about the themes in emotional disorders, it often takes little time to uncover the client's irrational self-talk. For example, with the client's problem discussed above, a possible ABC sequence might be:

Theme in anxiety: future danger or threat with self as vulnerable

A = When I am around people who are better educated than me, I think they will look down on me.

B = 'I must not be looked down on as being uneducated. If I am, it proves that I am an idiot.'

C = Anxiety.

Key Point

Obtain an ABC picture of the client's presenting problem, not a big picture of it.

6 Believing you need to understand the past before you can deal with the present

REBT focuses on how emotional problems are being perpetuated rather than on how they were acquired. You may believe that the present cannot be understood without reference to the past as the latter continually influences the former (e.g. 'Clients cannot easily dump or ignore their historical baggage'). We would argue that you can understand the past through the lens of the present by uncovering your clients' *current* thinking about past events and thereby understand how they continue to disturb themselves about these events:

Client: I still feel miserable about my husband dumping me ten years ago. He's caused me all this misery.

[The client clearly blames her husband for her ten years of misery.]

Therapist: It's certainly unpleasant to be dumped, but what have you been telling yourself (tapping forehead) all these years to continue the misery?

Client: Who wants to be dumped?

Therapist: Probably no one, but others who have been dumped have picked up the pieces and found new partners. You haven't done that.

[The therapist is pointing out that she had choices about adjusting to being dumped.]

Client: How could I have done? He made me feel worthless when he dumped me. Who else would want me?

Therapist: Let's say he did try to make you feel worthless; did you agree that you were worthless?

[The therapist is pointing out that the client is the ultimate judge of her self-appraisal.]

Client: I suppose I did.

Therapist: What have you been telling yourself for the last ten years and what do you continue to tell yourself?

Client: I'm worthless.

Therapist: Is seeing yourself as worthless why you believe no one else will want you?

Client: (quietly) Yes.

Exploring the client's past will probably prolong her present distress; so,

> the crucial thing is for him or her to give up these currently held ideas so that tomorrow's existence can be better than yesterday's. In a sense, the person each day chooses to either hold onto disturbed beliefs or to give them up (Grieger and Boyd, 1980: 76–7).

Some clients will be preoccupied with past events. These events will often need to be explored before they can focus on their present difficulties (looking back is not contra-indicated in REBT as long as you do not dwell there). This historical quest will involve you helping your clients to uncover their past beliefs about past events. For example, a client who has left her partner (e.g. 'He was a loser') wonders: 'What did I ever see in him in the first place?' By mentally travelling back to when she first met him, you can help her to elicit her thinking about herself at that time (e.g. 'I needed someone, anyone, to love me. A life without love was awful'). Going out with him met her needs at that time (just because she has a different self-image and expectations today does not make her partner a 'loser' – just someone following his own goals).

Key Point

Explore past events through clients' current thinking about these events. However, there might be times when you need to uncover past beliefs about past events.

---

7 Wanting to give clients opportunities to express themselves in their own way instead of through the REBT model

When clients start therapy, they understandably want to talk about their problems in their own way. Another frame of reference for this self-exploration has not yet been offered to them. Once you start teaching clients about REBT, it is important to encourage them to shift from unstructured to structured self-exploration through the use of the ABC model. However, some trainees continue to give clients opportunities to talk about themselves in non-REBT ways:

Supervisor: Listening to your session tape, you don't appear to bring any structure to the session.

Trainee: What do you mean? I don't understand.

Supervisor: You are letting your client express herself in her own way, which has nothing to do with the REBT way.

Trainee: But I thought that's what therapy is all about: letting clients express things in their own terms.

Supervisor: Some therapies see it that way, but how are clients ever going to learn REBT, if you don't encourage them to use it?

Trainee: Well, I suppose it's forcing REBT-speak on them. I don't fancy doing that.

Supervisor: You are not forcing anything on clients but offering them a model within which to understand and explore their problems. They can use their own language, as long as it reflects REBT concepts.

Trainee: I suppose I still see it as forcing clients into REBT instead of seeing it as offering REBT to them. Thinking about it now, it's silly: I'm training in REBT, but I encourage clients to behave as if I'm not training in it.

Supervisor: Exactly. Also, how do you know that clients will profit more from exploring problems in their own ways instead of through the ABC model?

Trainee: I suppose I don't – it's just my assumption.

Supervisor: And what do we do with assumptions in REBT?

Trainee: Test them out. So, in my next session tapes, you will want to hear my clients talking about their problems in ABC terms. Right?

Supervisor: Right.

Key Point

Encourage your clients to express themselves in a structured, REBT-focused way.

8 Listening passively

You might believe you are actively listening to the client's problems because you are nodding your head, producing a string of 'hmms' or using seemingly empathic words such as 'Sure', 'Right' or 'Absolutely' and employing paraphrasing, reflecting and summarizing as part of your listening skills. We would suggest that, in REBT terms, this is passive, not active, listening. Active listening in REBT is being on the alert for the ABC components of clients' presenting problems: this 'search for the ABCs of client problems begins the moment the person enters therapy' (Grieger and Boyd, 1980: 59). In this dialogue excerpt, the trainee is *not* listening for the ABC components:

Client: Yeah, I mean, it's always the same: my boss always asks for my opinion last at the meeting. I'm sure everyone wonders why he does it. Why does he keep on doing this to me? I'm not happy about it at all. I work hard; I'm not a slacker. It affects me for the rest of the morning. He must have it in for me, got to pick on someone I suppose. He probably gets a tough time from his manager; so he's got to find a cat to kick – and I'm it!

Trainee: Doesn't sound like a nice guy.

Client: He's not that popular, I can tell you.

[The client goes on to explore at some length the psychology of his boss. The trainee's generally supportive comments reinforce in the client's mind that the focus of therapy is his boss's behaviour.]

In this extract, the therapist, through active listening, starts building an initial ABC conceptualization of the client's problem:

Therapist: The problem or A in this model is your boss always asking you last at the meeting for your opinion. Is that correct?

Client: That's right.

Therapist: Now, at C, which stands for emotional and behavioural consequences, you said, 'I'm not happy about it all.' If you're not happy about it, then how do you actually feel?

19

['Not happy' reflects the client's affective response to his boss's behaviour.]

Client: Mightily pissed off.

Therapist: Does that mean angry?

[The therapist wants to clarify the client's statement to ensure an unhealthy negative emotion has been revealed.]

Client: Yes, very. It screwed up the rest of my morning.

Therapist: That was after the meeting, but to return to the model: we have got the A and C elements. Now we need to find out what you were telling yourself at B in order to make yourself angry at C. You said 'Why does he keep on doing this to me?' Is this asked with genuine uncertainty or does it have its own answer?

[Clients often phrase their irrational ideas in rhetorical questions, and it is important to transform them into straightforward statements.]

Client: He shouldn't do this to me at the meetings. He's an obnoxious bastard. I'd like to wring his scrawny neck!

[What was implicit has now been made explicit. Whether it is the most important anger-producing belief (B) can be determined after an examination of it.]

Cormier and Cormier define listening 'as involving three processes: receiving a message, processing a message, and sending a message' (1985: 89). In REBT terms, receiving a message is the client's account of her problems, processing the message is assembling an ABC structure of her problems in your mind, and sending a message is presenting this structure to the client for her consideration and comment. Active listening requires your sustained concentration and direct questioning in each and every session; passive listening is more of an invitation to let your thoughts or the client's wander in each and every session.

Key Point

Keep your REBT 'radar' always switched on in order to detect the ABC components of clients' presenting difficulties. Active listening is required from the first to the last session.

9 Not ensuring that the client has answered the questions you have asked

When you ask a question, you presumably want an answer. REBTers ask direct questions in order to elicit specific information from their clients (e.g. 'How did you feel when you did not get the promotion' or 'What were you thinking when you made that mistake in front of your colleagues?'). An error we frequently encounter among novice REBT therapists is not obtaining an answer to a question they have asked. For example:

Trainee: What prevents you from getting to the sessions on time?

Client: Lateness.

[Lateness is the consequence, not the cause, of the client's poor timekeeping.]

Trainee: Could you try to be on time for the next session?

Client: I'll do my best.

The trainee did not get an answer to his question, and the problem of the client's habitual lateness remains unexplored. The trainee could have stuck to his guns:

Trainee: What prevents you from getting to the sessions on time?

Client: Lateness.

Trainee: Obviously you're late, but that doesn't explain what prevented you from getting here on time. What does?

Client: I leave it to the last minute before I come here.

Trainee: Why do you do that?

Client: Because I'm in two minds about coming here. It's touch and go whether I'll come or not.

[The trainee has finally got an answer to his original question and then explores the client's ambivalent attitude towards therapy.]

Clients will frequently give you thoughts when you ask them for feelings. These cognitions are usually prefaced by the words 'I feel' and thereby create the impression that your questions have been answered. This is not the case. You are looking for an unhealthy negative emotion (e.g. depression, anger, guilt) connected to your client's thoughts about the activating event:

Trainee: How did you feel when your husband shouted at you?

Client: I felt that this was the end of our marriage.

Trainee: That was a thought, not a feeling. How did you feel?

Client: I felt that everything I worked for was in ruins.

Trainee: Okay, you're giving me thoughts, and we will examine those in a minute. Now feelings are usually captured in one word like 'anger' or 'anxiety'. More than one word is usually a thought. So how did you feel in your gut when your husband shouted at you?

[The trainee explains a distinction between thoughts and feelings as part of his attempt to get an answer to his question. He uses the evocative 'in your gut' as further encouragement to reveal her feelings.]

Client: Angry and hurt.

Clients often respond to questions with 'I don't know'. You may wonder how you are supposed to obtain answers to this reply. If you accept such replies without further enquiry, this will help to maintain clients' ignorance about their problems instead of promoting insight into them. In this dialogue excerpt, the therapist asks questions in order to discover what the client does know:

Therapist: When you are angry when you speak to your mother on the phone, are you angry with yourself or your mother?

Client: I get angry with myself when I speak to my mother on the phone, but I don't know why.

Therapist: Is it a particular subject you are going to touch on or something else?

[The therapist's question hopes to stimulate the client's thinking.]

Client: My hackles start to rise when my mother asks me about my relationship with Caroline.

[The relationship seems to be an entry point into the client's anger.]

Therapist: Because . . . ?

Client: My relationship with Caroline is falling apart. She's seeing someone else I think, but I tell my mother everything is fine.

Therapist: But, if you told her that everything wasn't fine . . . ?

Client: Then I'd feel a complete failure. I can't even hold a relationship together. I'm pathetic.

[This appears to be the core of the client's anger with himself. The therapist seeks confirmation of this.]

Therapist: So are you angry with yourself for not being able to hold the relationship together and this makes you a 'failure, pathetic' in your mind? (client nods) Is speaking to your mother a painful reminder of this?

Client: Yes. That's why I try not to phone her too often.

See 'I don't know' as a challenge, rather than as a block, in order to bring the information, which is currently outside of your client's awareness, into your client's awareness. Asking questions is not a form of interrogation that is supposed to put clients on the defensive but a means of stimulating greater introspective awareness of their disturbance-inducing patterns of thinking.

Key Point

When your questions have not been answered, bring this to your clients' attention, and then help them to answer these questions.

10 Not interrupting rambling or verbose clients

REBT views interrupting such clients as necessary rather than impolite, but make sure you explain the reasons for your interruptions. Only some aspects of what clients talk about is clinically significant from an REBT perspective (remaining silent creates the impression that everything they say is significant and you want to hear all of it). Valuable therapy time can be wasted through not reining in your overly talkative clients as in the following extract:

Trainee: What were you anxious about with regard to your best friend's divorce?

[The trainee's question puts the focus squarely on the client's subjective responses to the divorce.]

Client: Well, they've had such a great relationship. Who would have guessed it would have ended in divorce? The perfect couple, we all said so. But what goes on behind closed doors? That's the question. Obviously, she's in a state over it. I expect he is too – he was a nice bloke, you know – but I haven't seen him since the separation. She says that she'll never get over it. Time heals, that's what I say. You know the divorce rate seems to go up all the time. I suppose none of us is safe; that's what worries me. Are you married or shouldn't I ask that? I suppose I'm here to talk about me, not you. Isn't that right?

As well as not answering the question, most of what the client said is neither relevant nor illuminating. After listening to a few of the client's responses, the trainee could have asked: 'You're talking about them, but what I need to know is, and I'll ask you again, what were *you* anxious about with regard to their divorce?' Another intervention point to direct the client's attention to was when she briefly hinted at what might be troubling her: 'I suppose none of us is safe, that's what worries me':

Therapist: What are you worried about, whether no one is safe?

Client: It could happen to me.

Therapist: Do you mean divorce? (client nods) And, if it did happen to you . . . ?

Client: (becomes tearful) My life would be destroyed.

Therapist: Is that what you were anxious about in regard to your friend's divorce? (client nods)

You may be reluctant to interrupt your clients because you fear that by doing so you will damage them or the relationship. Treat your fears as hypotheses to be tested. If some clients do become upset when you interrupt them, elicit their thoughts (e.g. 'I feel you're not really interested in me. I'm just another head case to deal with') and show them that it is their appraisals of the interruptions that leads to their upset feelings, not the interruption itself (though interrupting insensitively contributes to the client being upset). With regard to your interruptions damaging the relationship, interruptions, among other activities, provide you with evidence to gauge the strength of the relationship, while not interrupting is more likely to reinforce your untested assumption that you have such a relationship.

Trainees often complain to us that one of the major reasons they do not interrupt verbose clients is because they are not sure when to (e.g. 'How do I know whether the client is giving me too much information or going off at a tangent?'). We would suggest a simple rule of thumb to help you with these clients: are you able to make ABC sense from what the client is saying? If not, interrupt to clarify and cut through the verbiage:

Therapist: I'm having trouble understanding what the problem is for you with regard to your brother-in-law. You've given me so much information. Could you put it in a nutshell for me?

Client: He waves all his wealth in my face. Arrogant bastard.

[The client has presented an A and hinted at a C.]

Therapist: It sounds like you are angry about that. Are you?

Client: I am.

[The therapist's hypothesis about the C is confirmed.]

Therapist: What are you angry about when he waves all his wealth in your face?

Client: He makes me feel like a loser because I have a poorly paid job.

Therapist: Do you see yourself as a 'loser' because you have a poorly paid job or him waving his wealth in your face?

[The therapist is seeking the most relevant A, as well as emphasizing emotional responsibility in the way she has structured the question.]

Client: I see myself as a loser for having a poorly paid job.

[The client has confirmed a B – self-depreciation.]

Therapist: So is this your view of yourself irrespective of how your brother-in-law behaves?

Client: Yes, but his behaviour doesn't help, does it?

Key Point

Long-windedness is the antithesis of efficient therapy; so interrupt tactfully to concentrate the client's mind on the salient aspects of his difficulties.

11 Being verbose

This can occur when you present REBT concepts in large chunks, ask too many questions or lack verbal conciseness. This time the shoe is on the other foot, and the client feels confused or overwhelmed by your verbal onslaught:

Trainee: I'm wondering why you can now stay in those situations where before you used to avoid them for fear of panic attacks. Obviously you're making progress; so it's important to find out what's going on. Comparing now with then helps to provide us with information on changes you're making. So I wonder what's going on with you now. Can you put it in your own words and describe it for me? What are you telling yourself, in other words?

[All the trainee had to ask was: 'How are you now able to stay in those situations that you used to avoid?']

Client: I'm not sure what you're asking me.

Trainee: Well, I'm trying to find out what you're telling yourself about those situations now that you weren't telling yourself about those situations several weeks ago. You're behaving differently, aren't you? You're probably feeling differently too. So what I'm getting at is pinpointing a 'change scenario' within you.

[The trainee could have said: 'You no longer panic in those situations; so what has changed within you?']

Client: I know I probably sound thick, but I still don't quite understand what you want from me.

A client's ability to think through her problems and solutions to them usually varies in inverse ratio to the amount of talking that you do. More of her time is spent struggling to understand what you are talking about and less of it on examining her own thought processes.

Trainee verbosity can also stem from anxiety: your demand to 'get it right' every time you open your mouth, i.e. your questions and comments must have textbook precision. Instead of refining each question or comment in the light of the client's responses, you attempt to refine it too much before offering it to the client, thereby baffling her (as in the above dialogue) and often yourself. We advise you to get rid of your verbal clutter and to practise verbal economy or asking short questions, one at a time (you may be surprised how often clients now understand what you have asked them).

Key Point

Make your communication with clients clear, concise and direct.

---

12 Failing to obtain feedback

Feedback enables you to determine the client's level of understanding of and agreement with REBT concepts, his progress and stumbling blocks, his reactions to therapy and the therapist – this information is gleaned as part of REBT's open and collaborative approach to problem solving. Not obtaining feedback suggests the client's views are unimportant and can turn him into a passive (and possibly resentful) partner in therapy. Feedback requires specific information; nods, paraverbal responses, one-word replies or general comments are valueless:

Trainee: I've been explaining how REBT sees the differences between self-acceptance and self-esteem. Do you understand the differences?

Client: Yeah.

['Yeah' could mean any number of things: understanding, lack of understanding, misunderstanding, boredom, irritation, compliance.]

Trainee: Good. Now let's move on to how you practise self-acceptance.

The client's reply of 'Yeah' should have been the starting point for clarification:

Therapist: I'm not sure what 'Yeah' means. Could you explain what these differences are?

Client: Well, self-acceptance is about not putting yourself down under any circumstances, while, with the self-esteem thing, you're more likely to put yourself down when things go against you.

[Understanding is not synonymous with agreement or indicating usefulness, so further feedback is sought.]

Therapist: That's a good way of putting it. Do you think that self-acceptance could be more helpful to you than sticking with self-esteem? (the client shrugs his shoulders)

Therapist: What does that mean?

[The client's gesture suggests that more information needs to be elicited by the therapist.]

Client: Well, it's all right being self-accepting, but you still want to get on in life. Self-acceptance sounds like you just sit around all day saying 'I can accept myself', but so what? Big deal. At least with self-esteem you're pushing yourself to succeed, make something of yourself.

[Feedback has revealed the client's misunderstanding of self-acceptance and presented the therapist with an opportunity to correct it. Lack of feedback in the previous dialogue extract may have meant the client carrying this misunderstanding throughout the course of therapy and thereby reinforcing his adherence to the conditional self-acceptance of self-esteem.]

Therapist: Thanks for that feedback. That's not what I meant by self-acceptance. I may have explained it wrongly. Let me try again: self-acceptance is the basis for striving to reach your goals in life but without condemning yourself when you encounter setbacks or failures along the way. Has that made it clearer?

Client: I like the way you've explained it now. That picture of self-acceptance will be helpful to me. It's not a sitting-on-your-backside approach to life.

[The client's motivation for change based on self-acceptance has been activated.]

The same process applies to end-of-session feedback: when you ask 'What was helpful and unhelpful about today's session?', ensure the client's responses are clear and specific.

Key Point

Obtain clear and concrete feedback from your clients on a regular basis.

13 Avoiding confrontation

Confrontation can be seen as in-your-face aggression, arguing, power struggles and general nastiness towards someone else. In REBT, confrontation means acting assertively

> when the therapist detects discrepancies (a) between what the clients are saying and what they have said before, (b) between what the clients are communicating verbally and nonverbally, and (c) between the way the clients view their problem and the way the therapist views it. Confrontation in counseling is particularly encouraged when the therapist notes discrepancies in the client's thoughts, feelings, and actions (Walen et al., 1992: 61).

Novice therapists often avoid confrontation because, among other reasons, they see it (wrongly) as a form of bullying, they prefer to seek comfort in therapy or they believe confrontation will lead to some perceived catastrophe (e.g. the client storming out of the room). Confrontation brings to the client's attention issues that need addressing, but the trainee backs away from it in this excerpt from therapy:

Trainee: I'm puzzled by something: you say you want to repair your damaged relationship with your wife, but most of your concern is based on discussing how she will cope if you leave her. Do you want to repair the relationship or leave her?

Client: (fiercely) Are you trying to be clever or something?

[The client's response indicates the trainee has ventured into a sensitive area.]

Trainee: No, no, I didn't mean any disrespect. I apologize for that. Let's discuss something else. How are things at work?

Client: I'm prepared to discuss that.

31

By backtracking, the trainee has demonstrated to the client that he will now steer clear of 'hot button' issues, and the client knows how to 'scare' him away, if he becomes curious again. Not backing away produces a different outcome:

Therapist: I'm not trying to be clever. You seem to have two agendas: the first is telling me you want to repair your relationship, and the second, which appears to be the real one, is your planning to leave her.

Client: That's bollocks!

Therapist: It may be bollocks, but why do you spend so much time worrying about how she will cope if you leave her? Can you explain that to me?

Client: (sighs deeply) I don't know. Maybe I do want to leave her. I'd feel guilty if I did because I know she'd go to pieces.

Therapist: Shall we now focus on this issue?

Client: (quietly) Yes. It's tearing me apart inside.

You can seek feedback to discover the impact of your confrontational stance upon the client and the consequences for the therapeutic alliance:

Client: It was an issue that needed to be brought out into the open.

Therapist: Has it damaged our relationship in some way by me confronting you about this issue?

Client: I don't think so. Are you going to be like this all the time?

Therapist: Only when I think something really needs to be discussed and you appear to be avoiding it. Okay?

Client: Okay.

Always provide reasons for your challenging behaviour, otherwise you are likely to be perceived by your clients as too confrontational (Dryden, 1995).

Key Point

Do not avoid confrontation: it is an assertive means of highlighting inconsistencies and contradictions in clients' statements.

14 Not working collaboratively

REBT stresses collaboration: therapist and client working together to tackle the latter's problem. You can only go as far and as fast as the client allows. Unfortunately, some trainees forget to seek the co-operation of their clients and direct therapy unilaterally. This non-collaborative stance may occur because, among other reasons, you overwhelm your clients with your enthusiasm for REBT or you are mainly didactic in your approach as you have read in the REBT literature that therapists are authoritative teachers of emotional disturbance and its remediation. While the goal of REBT therapists is to help their clients achieve emotional change through cognitive restructuring, how this is achieved is of crucial importance for the success of therapy:

Supervisor: Listening to your tape, do you think you're working collaboratively with your client?

Trainee: I think so.

Supervisor: I think not. You told him which problem you were going to work on instead of asking him. He seemed to me to be rather irritated with your choice.

Trainee: Well, I thought we are supposed to work on the worst aspect of the client's problem first. The elegant solution and all that. He's hardly going to like it, is he?

Supervisor: He doesn't have to like the elegant solution, but he needs to be consulted by you about pursuing it and his agreement must be sought. Now, are you collaborating on agenda setting and homework tasks, for example?

Trainee: (sheepishly) No. I keep forgetting in my enthusiasm to help him get over his problems as quickly as possible.

Supervisor: It's good that you're enthusiastic, but he might see it as coercion or see himself as a puppet with you pulling the strings. So what do we need to hear on your next session tape?

Trainee: Me working collaboratively.

Supervisor: Good. Hearing his viewpoint as well as yours.

Key Point

Collaboration means the active engagement of your clients in the problem-solving process.

15 Not adopting a problem-orientated focus

A problem-orientated focus means not only asking for a problem and then working on it but also dealing with *any* difficulty that arises in therapy. A problem-orientated outlook should be your natural stance in therapy. You may 'switch off' such an outlook, if you believe you are not directly dealing with a problem:

Client: My company is sending me to the Scotland office for a couple of months; so I won't be able to come to therapy. I think that two months is too long before our next session.

Trainee: Well, that's unfortunate, but maybe you could see how you cope being your own self-therapist, and we'll review your progress in a couple of months' time. How does that sound?

[The trainee could have asked why the client sees a two-month hiatus in therapy as 'too long' or what worries she has about the temporary separation. Seeing the separation as an experiment is an attempt to 'smooth over' the client's concerns.]

Client: (frowning) Hmm.

[The client is not convinced.]

Trainee: You're probably making a mountain out of a molehill; so let's pick up this discussion in two months' time.

The client could have been upset because the separation was enforced by her company instead of agreed by her. A stopgap measure would have been to schedule telephone counselling sessions. Working on the principle that everything that happens in therapy is grist to the cognitive mill, the therapist in this dialogue does not try to smooth things over:

Client: Why did you look at your watch as if you can't wait to get rid of me?

Therapist: I simply looked at my watch to see how much time we had left. Obviously, you see it in a different way. What does it mean to you, if I can't wait to get rid of you?

[The therapist wants to pursue the implications of the client's inference.]

Client: You too see me as a boring misery guts.

Therapist: Do you believe that this is a generally held impression of you?

Client: Yes, I do. People tell me that I am.

Therapist: I genuinely haven't got the time today to discuss this issue in depth, but shall we put it on the agenda for the next session?

[The therapist does not want to start exploring this issue then call a halt a few minutes later; so she suggests it as an agenda item for the next session so it won't be overlooked.]

Client: (nodding) Okay.

Key Point

A problem-orientated focus is constant, not intermittent.

16 Failing to keep clients on track

Your clients might view therapy as an extension of their everyday conversations: shooting off in all directions as the mood takes them. Indeed, such verbal behaviour is expected from clients (as well as the rest of us). In REBT, the talk needs to be structured and focused, if progress is to be made with the client's target problem. As we discussed in Point 10, it is important to interrupt clients tactfully if they meander or are verbose. In this extract, the client leaves the track and the trainee follows him:

Trainee: You say you have an explosive temper, can you give me a recent example when your temper exploded?

Client: Yesterday. My boss cancelled a meeting with me at the last minute. I was wild. My wife says that if I don't get my anger under control, I'm going to end up in prison, seriously ill or dead. I know she's right, but it's so hard to change my behaviour.

[The client has not explained why he went 'wild' when his boss cancelled the meeting.]

Trainee: I think your wife has a very good point. Shall we explore how anger is linked to illness?

[The trainee does not bring the client back to the 'I went wild' episode for an ABC understanding of it. How anger is linked to illness is useful to explore but not at this point.]

Client: Okay.

[The rest of the session is used for discussing illness-related issues.]

When clients do go off track, it may be useful sometimes to examine the clinical relevance of the new information presented in order to determine whether to stay with the present issue or discuss this new information

37

(e.g. a client feels ashamed when discussing her panic attacks and becomes preoccupied with these shameful feelings; at this point, the clinical focus is switched from panic to shame as further progress with the former problem cannot be made until the latter one is addressed). If you do choose to go off track, then stay on track in examining these new data!

Key Point

Keep your clients on track (i.e. problem focused) when discussing their problems.

---

17 Not checking clients' understanding of REBT terminology

REBT has its own specialist terminology, which needs to be explained to your clients, a non-specialist group. Such terms would include 'irrational', 'awfulizing', 'emotional and therapeutic responsibility' and 'unhealthy and healthy negative emotions'. You can view REBT terms as As that clients may misinterpret because they have their own meanings of these terms (Dryden and Yankura, 1995). So you might be using the same word but in very different ways:

Trainee: You're thinking irrationally when you say that your daughter should have come home at the time you stated.

[The trainee needs to explain what she means by the term 'irrational'.]

Client: How am I thinking irrationally? Am I really being unbalanced because I want my daughter to come home at a reasonable time?

[The client has interpreted 'irrational' as 'being unbalanced'.]

Trainee: Well, when you are thinking irrationally, you don't see how the situation actually is because you are not looking at the evidence.

[The trainee has not specifically countered the client's view of irrationality.]

Client: I do see how the situation actually is: something bad could happen to my daughter if she stays out all night. You seem to think I'm a case for the loony bin because I'm being irrational.

[The trainee has failed to explain 'irrational' in a way that is intelligible to the client because he still views its meaning as being mentally unbalanced. Unless this confusion over irrational is resolved, it could lead to a rift in the therapeutic relationship.]

When you use REBT terms, automatically explain what you mean by them and what you do not mean by them and then check whether the client has understood what you have explained to him:

Therapist: When I use the term 'irrational', I mean that your view of the situation – what your daughter should do – does not conform with the actual facts: she doesn't come home at the time you state. There's a mismatch between your view of the situation and the reality. Can you explain in your own words what I mean by irrational?

Client: Well, that my view of things is not necessarily the way things actually are. So does that make me unbalanced then?

Therapist: The REBT view of irrational does not mean unbalanced, unhinged, mad or have any other psychiatric connection.

Client: Okay, so I'm thinking irrationally but I'm not unbalanced. Right, so how do I make my daughter come home on time?

[The client's use of 'make my daughter' sounds like more irrational thinking; so the therapist would need to return to discussing REBT's view of irrationality.]

Other REBT terms that are commonly misunderstood by clients include 'self-acceptance' (e.g. encouraging passivity, complacency, selfishness, and not striving for life goals), 'rational' (e.g. being emotionless, cold, aloof, icily detached, always logical) and 'high frustration tolerance' (e.g. maintaining a stiff upper lip at all times). Checking that your clients understand REBT terms correctly is not a one-off procedure but needs your attention throughout the course of therapy (see my [WD] book, 1995, for correcting misconceptions about REBT).

Key Point

When you use REBT terminology, explain what these terms mean; then ascertain from your clients their understanding of your explanation of these terms.

18 Not developing a shared vocabulary

Some clients may find REBT terminology not to their particular tastes and will want to use their own personally meaningful terms. This is fine, as long as their terms reflect REBT concepts – a crucial point. Unfortunately, you may be so theory-bound that you insist on your clients using REBT terms or, in your haste to teach REBT, fail to ask whether they have alternative terms they would prefer to use. For example, I (MN) used the term 'low frustration tolerance' (LFT) to refer to a client's avoidance of a situation where he would experience intense discomfort; the client replied indignantly that he did not have LFT but 'lacked the courage' to enter the situation. Both LFT and 'lacked the courage' referred to discomfort anxiety but only 'lacked the courage' was used from then on. In the following dialogue, the trainee has explained the REBT distinction between unhealthy and healthy negative emotions (e.g. anxiety vs. concern respectively). The client prefers to use her own term, 'confident', as a healthy alternative to anxiety:

Client: Feeling confident would be great. I wouldn't have that stomach-churning anxiety when running workshops.

Trainee: Sounds good. Let's work on developing that.

By not analysing what 'feeling confident' actually means, the trainee and her client could now be pursuing different emotional goals instead of a common one. In this dialogue, the therapist teases out the client's meaning of confidence:

Client: Feeling confident means things going really well. My workshops are successful, I can answer all the questions, always give a good performance, that sort of thing.

Therapist: Does it allow for performance or workshop failures? That you have the confidence to tackle these things when they occur?

41

Client: I don't want any failures. That's why I want to feel confident. My anxiety was about failing, and I dreaded that.

[It is clear that feeling confident is not underpinned by rational ideas but by positive or wishful thinking.]

Therapist: Unless feeling confident also includes coping with setbacks and failures, you're likely to start feeling anxious again the first workshop hiccup you have. You cannot abolish failure from your mind or life by telling yourself you will now feel confident. If you will pardon the pun, that is a confidence trick you're playing on yourself. Do you want your confidence to be built on solid or fragile foundations?

Client: Okay, that makes sense. What now?

[The therapist then explains in more detail the rational principles underlying feeling confident and whether it is to be considered a genuinely healthy and adaptive emotion.]

Key Point

Ensure that, whatever terms are jointly agreed, they reflect REBT concepts.

---

19 Trying to teach B–C thinking while struggling unsuccessfully to abandon A–C language

Clients use A–C language when describing their problems (e.g. 'My partner makes me angry when he ignores me'), while your task is to teach B–C thinking (e.g. 'I make myself angry when my partner ignores me'). B–C thinking is probably alien to many clients but essential for them to adopt if they want to develop greater emotional stability in their lives. In our experience, trainees often have great difficulty in trying not to lapse into A–C language, while simultaneously attempting to talk in B–C terms and restructuring clients' statements into the same terms. This juggling act can lead to all sorts of muddle:

Client: Meeting new people makes me anxious.

[A clear A–C statement.]

Trainee: Now what are you anxious about when you meet new people that they make you anxious?

[The trainee should have stopped after 'people' as this is a B–C question, but he finishes with an A–C one.]

Client: They make me feel nervous.

Trainee: They're not responsible for the way you feel. How do you make yourself nervous when you meet them? What are you saying to yourself to feel nervous? Your nervousness is created by you, not by them. So what do they do to produce this nervousness in you?

[The trainee delivers a B–C onslaught but does not check his language carefully enough in the last question. These mixed A–C and B–C messages cannot but confuse the client.]

Client: Let me get this straight: I'm responsible for making myself nervous when I meet new people, but they're responsible too. Right?

You may struggle with B–C thinking for some of the following reasons: you still have reservations about emotional responsibility (can it apply in all cases?), you were an A-C thinker before studying REBT (along with the majority of the population) and find it is a hard habit to break, and, in your anxiety to 'get it right' (see Point 11), A–C and B–C statements struggle for supremacy in your mind with the outcome frequently changing between questions (i.e. you teach B–C thinking with one question but let the client 'off the hook' with the next one). In the following dialogue, the therapist ensures that her statements and questions reinforce REBT's position that B primarily determines C, not A:

Therapist: What are you anxious about when you meet new people?

Client: They make me anxious.

Therapist: Meeting new people doesn't have to be anxiety provoking unless you are telling yourself something anxiety provoking up here (tapping forehead). So what are you telling yourself?

[The therapist keeps the search for the source of the client's anxiety internally focused.]

Client: They might not like me.

Therapist: What would it mean about you, if they didn't like you?

Client: That I'm unlikeable. There's something wrong with me.

Therapist: If you saw yourself as likeable, there was nothing wrong with you, would meeting new people make you anxious?

[This question seeks to show the client that his self-evaluation is the key to his emotional response when he meets new people.]

Client: No.

Therapist: Because . . . ?

Client: Because I wouldn't worry what they thought of me.

Therapist: So who makes you anxious or not anxious when you meet new people?

Client: I do. Okay, case proven.

When you become adept at using B–C language, show some restraint in not correcting your clients every time they use A–C language, as this can come across as nit-picking or pedantic. Select for correction clients' A–C statements that are central to their emotional problems.

Key Point

Ensure that you use only B–C language with your clients. Do not be too zealous in correcting your clients every time they lapse into A–C thinking.

---

20 Not socializing clients into REBT in the first or early sessions of therapy

Socializing clients into REBT means letting them know what is expected of them in this form of therapy. What is expected of them includes selecting a problem, goal setting, collaborating with the therapist on the problem-solving process, accepting emotional and therapeutic responsibility, understanding the crucial role of evaluative beliefs in determining their emotional reactions to events, disputing irrational beliefs, constructing rational beliefs and carrying out homework tasks. This socialization process also requires you to inform the client of your tasks. As I (WD) have said: 'When you prepare your clients to understand REBT and the roles that you and they have to play in the [therapy] process, they will make more effective use of therapy' (1994: 22). Lack of preparation may mean your clients are confused or resentful about the tasks you keep 'piling on them':

Client: I didn't have to do homework tasks in my previous therapy.

Trainee: This is a very different type of therapy. In REBT, you put into daily practice what you learn in these sessions.

Client: It seems that in every session there is something new for me to do. I thought when I came here I could just talk about whatever I wanted and you got me better.

If you have over looked the socialization process at the beginning of REBT, then carrying it out belatedly is better than not carrying it out at all:

Trainee: REBT is very structured; so there is quite a bit for you to do. The talk needs to be focused on obtaining information that I need in order to understand your problems in REBT terms. We work together, collaborate, on tackling your problems. You have your tasks to carry out and I have mine. I apologize for not explaining to you at the beginning of therapy what these would be.

Client: That might have helped. It would have let me know what I was letting myself in for.

Explaining to clients at the outset of REBT what tasks they will be required to execute allows them to make an informed decision whether or not to proceed with this form of therapy. Before this decision, clients are consumers; after it, having chosen to proceed, they become clients. Socialization is part of 'selling' REBT to clients as an effective treatment for psychological disorders. Bungle the 'selling' part and clients will probably be less interested in the 'product'.

Key Point

Do not socialize your clients into REBT in a piecemeal fashion; ensure that proper socialization is one of your primary tasks in the early stages of therapy.

---

21 Not teaching the ABC model in a clear way

The ABCs of REBT teach clients the principle of mainly self-induced emotional disturbance. Clients who fail to grasp this essential principle may continue to blame others or events for their emotional problems and become bewildered when you start challenging their irrational beliefs. Therefore, it is of paramount importance that you teach the model in a clear way, if these difficulties are to be avoided. Unfortunately, some trainees teach the model in unhelpful ways: for example, too fast, too elaborately (e.g. add too much detail), confusingly (e.g. 'I think I've explained it the right way') and unconvincingly (e.g. 'Whether you believe it or not, that's what REBT says anyway'). In this extract, the trainee teaches the model in a fast and throwaway fashion:

Trainee: Imagine, at A, two men being rejected by the same woman they both wanted to go out with. Now, at C, they feel differently about it, one may be pissed off and the other depressed. The reason they feel differently, at C, is because of how they think about rejection, at B, not the rejection itself, at A. That's the ABC model. Okay?

Client: (shrugs his shoulders) Yeah, okay. If you say so.

[The trainee should ideally have obtained feedback. Clients invariably have some comments to make about the model: for many of them, it is a completely different way of viewing emotional causation. The trainee could have used a visual aid to assist the client's understanding of the model.]

In the following dialogue, the therapist is careful to keep the client in step with him as he teaches the model:

Therapist: (writing on the whiteboard) In this model, A stands for the activating event or what happens. Let's use an example of two men wanting to go out with the same woman. She rejects both of them, at A.

48

Now, at B or beliefs, one man believes he can't be happy in his life unless he goes out with her while the other man is unhappy about being rejected but knows he'll quickly get over it. Can you just recap the story so far?

Client: Well, both men want to go out with this woman, who rejects both of them. One man thinks he can't be happy without her and the other one is unhappy about being rejected but sees himself quickly getting over it.

Therapist: Excellent summary. Now, C stands for the emotional consequences. What emotions do you think each of these men will be experiencing, at C?

[The therapist wants to establish whether the client can work out for himself that different beliefs (B) about A lead to different emotions, at C.]

Client: The one who thinks he can't be happy without her will probably feel depressed, and the other one, who sees himself quickly getting over it, will be irritated or disappointed, something like that.

Therapist: So why do they feel differently at C, if they both suffered the same rejection at A?

Client: Because they are thinking differently at B (pointing at the whiteboard) about what happened at A. (pause) But what if they were both depressed at C, wouldn't that mean that A caused C?

Therapist: If they are both depressed, what's going on at B then?

Client: They probably both think they can't be happy without her.

Therapist: Correct. If twenty men were all depressed at C . . . ?

Client: The same thing – look at their thinking about A.

Therapist: When you are standing at B, looking at A, you have a number of choices as to how you think about or evaluate A. Your choice at B will largely determine your emotional reaction at C.

Client: That makes a lot of sense. I suppose people don't pay much attention to how they think about these things.

Therapist: In REBT, we pay a very great deal of attention to how people think about these things. Now, let's see how this model can be applied to your problems.

The above dialogue focused on teaching the thought–feeling link (also known as the general principle of emotional responsibility). The next step is to educate your clients about the crucial roles of irrational and rational beliefs (B) in producing, respectively, disturbed and non-disturbed emotional responses at C (also known as the specific principle of emotional responsibility). This is the order of teaching emotional responsibility I (MN) favour but I (WD) prefer to go straight to the specific form:

Therapist: (writing on the whiteboard) Now, at A, or the activating event in this model, two men are rejected by the woman they both want to go out with. One man holds a rigid belief (B) about the rejection: 'She absolutely shouldn't have rejected me, but, as she has, this proves I'm worthless.' The second man holds a flexible belief (B) about the rejection: 'I very much wanted to go out with her, but there is no reason why she must not reject me. I will not reject myself because she has.' Now, which man is more likely to feel depressed, at C, about the rejection and why?

Client: The first man is more likely to feel depressed, at C, because he has staked everything on going out with her. His opinion of himself is riding on her decision. It's as if his whole life depends on her going out with him.

Therapist: How might the second man feel, at C, after being rejected?

Client: Well, probably disappointed, a bit upset, something along those lines. Certainly not depressed like the first man.

Therapist: If they have suffered the same A, rejection, how come they do not have the same emotional reaction, at C?

Client: Because of their thinking, at B. That's the important part.

Therapist: That's right. In REBT, we teach clients that demands or rigid beliefs are more likely to lead to disturbed emotions like depression, while preferences or flexible beliefs are more likely to produce non-disturbed emotions like disappointment. Does that make any sense to you?

Client: It does because I know I've slipped into that rigid way of thinking. It's not helpful at all.

Therapist: Okay. Let's see how this model can be applied to your problems.

Teaching the ABC model occurs throughout therapy, not just in its early stages, as clients can easily drift back to A–C thinking or find examples where they believe the ABC model does not apply. Also, with some clients, you will want to teach a more sophisticated version of the basic model (e.g. that events at A are not only past ones but anticipated future adverse events, meta-emotional problems) in order to maintain their interest in the counselling process as well as counter their ideas that the model is simplistic and therefore cannot be used with 'complex' problems.

Key Point

Remember the ABC of teaching the ABCs of REBT: always be clear in your presentation of the model.

---

22 Being didactic with clients who would profit more from Socratic dialogue and vice versa

Socratic dialogue and didactic explanations are used to teach REBT concepts to clients. Some didactic explanation is inevitable (e.g. presenting REBT to clients), but the preferred method of client learning is through Socratic dialogue (i.e. encouraging your clients to grasp REBT principles). However, it is important to gauge which one of these teaching techniques is being profitably employed at any given moment in therapy. In this dialogue, the trainee is stuck in lecture mode:

Trainee: You see, people go around saying 'He/she/it makes me upset', when, in fact, it's much more complex than that. REBT's view is that we largely upset ourselves about others' behaviour or events by the beliefs that we hold about these things, not that these things make us directly upset. They contribute to it, of course, but don't cause it. This goes against the grain of how most people probably view their emotional difficulties. So the way to start understanding our emotional upsets is by tuning into our thinking? Okay so far?

Client: That seems reasonable to me: our thinking is the real culprit rather than the events themselves. I'm certainly willing to go along with that.

Trainee: Good. Now to go on from there . . .

[The client grasped succinctly the trainee's point. The trainee should have then switched to Socratic dialogue to encourage the client to think through his reply with regard to his own problems. Unfortunately, the trainee continues in lecture mode.]

Too much didacticism from you can force your clients into becoming passive, dependent learners (dependent on didactic 'hand-outs' from you) rather than encouraging them to be active, independent thinkers. As Grieger and Boyd observe: 'Do only as much lecturing/telling as necessary to induce clients to do their own thinking' (1980: 116).

When you are being didactic, present your explanations in small, digestible chunks instead of large indigestible slabs and, as always, check your client's understanding 'after a brief explanation or at points during a complex explanation' (Wessler and Wessler, 1980: 178).

Conversely, being excessively Socratic can lead some clients to feel frustrated as they cannot, at that point, think things through for themselves. These frustrations can be exacerbated by your 'teacher knows all' approach:

Trainee: What do you think you were telling yourself to make yourself angry about his comments?

Client: I don't know.

Trainee: Let me put it another way: what thoughts were going through your mind at that moment, in that situation, that led you to feel angry?

Client: I really don't know.

Trainee: You were telling yourself something which I think I can guess at. It's just a matter of putting your cognitive finger on it, so to speak. Why do you think you reacted in that way to his comments?

[At this point, the trainee could have been briefly didactic and explained (or reiterated) the thought–feeling link, and then suggested some typical anger-producing beliefs in order to stimulate the client's thinking: 'Do any of those beliefs strike a chord with you?']

Client: (irritated) Look, I don't know. If you know the answer, then spit it out!

Socratic dialogue is neither a form of mental torture nor an opportunity for you to be a know-all but a means of teaching clients to become independent problem solvers.

Key Point

Keep a constant eye on whether Socratic dialogue or didactic explanation is the best method at any given moment for guiding clients through REBT.

23 Being insufficiently repetitive in teaching REBT concepts

You might believe that once you have taught an REBT concept (e.g. awfulizing) to your client, checked her comprehension of the concept, it should 'sink in'; then you can move on to teaching the next concept. Even if your client does explain in her own words her understanding of the concept, it may not have made any impact upon her in terms of thinking, feeling or behaving differently. In this dialogue, the trainee seems surprised that the client 'hasn't got it yet':

Trainee: What demand were you making when you got angry about the queue moving so slowly?

Client: Well, I wanted the queue to move a bit quicker because I was in a hurry.

Trainee: Wants don't lead to disturbed feelings, demands do. We discussed demands at some length in the last session. Do you remember?

Client: I think so.

Trainee: Do you remember the importance I attached to demands and looking for them when you're upset?

Client: Er . . . I'm not sure.

Trainee: We did go over this, you know.

[Instead of keep asking the client whether she remembers last session's teaching of the role of demands in emotional disturbance (she clearly does not) the trainee should start teaching the same message again and again – as many times as it takes for the point to really 'sink in'.]

Repeating REBT ideas does not have to be a monotonous affair but, instead, can provide you with opportunities to display your creativity (see my (WD) book, 1990).

> ## Key Point
> Repeat REBT principles until they become part of your client's rational outlook.

24 Not explaining the purpose of an intervention

Explaining the purpose of an intervention before you proceed with it may seem self-evident. Unfortunately, some trainees, in their haste to help clients, execute an intervention without providing a rationale for it. An unexpected intervention can come as an unpleasant surprise to clients and show a lack of sensitivity on your part. For example, Ellis (1979) advocates the use of force and energy in disputing clients' irrational beliefs, but not without preparing the client for this approach – something the trainee has forgotton in this extract:

Trainee: (vigorously) Why must you have other people's approval?

Client: (hesitantly) I suppose . . . well . . . I . . . er . . . just feel that I do.

Trainee: Where's the evidence that you must have it, not just want it, but must have it? That you can't live without it?

Client: I don't like it when people don't like me. It makes life more difficult for me.

Trainee: (insistently) Where's the evidence you must have this approval, even if your life is made more difficult without it?

Client: I really don't know. Why are you treating me like this? I feel as though I'm in a police station.

Do not rely on a post-intervention explanation to justify your previously unexplained behaviour (e.g. 'Now can you see why I was being tough on you?') or expect the client to be automatically mollified by it (e.g. 'I still think you were out of order').

Key Point

Before an intervention, explain the purpose of it; after its execution, obtain feedback.

Part II:
Assessment Errors

25 Allowing clients to provide too much detail about the activating event

When clients talk about adverse events in their lives, it is understandable why some of them might provide you with a great amount of detail about these events (e.g. 'I want to get it out of my system'). However, they can overwhelm you with this mass of detail as well as lose themselves within it. This usually happens because you allow clients to talk endlessly about their As through, for example, your silence or active encouragement instead of directing their attention to the salient aspects of A. In this extract, the client believes everything is important to relate and is not disabused of this idea by the trainee:

Trainee: What problem would you like to discuss?

Client: Where do I begin? I was driving to work the other day and as usual got stuck in a traffic jam. Nowhere to go but lots of time to think, you know what I mean? (trainee nods). Anyway, I got to work and parked the car, walked up the stairs to my office – I try to avoid taking the lift because I want to be fitter – and sat down at my desk. I got myself a coffee from the machine first. Need that coffee surge to get me into gear, know what I mean? Loads of emails, and they all want something from you, always on your case. I'm sure you have the same problem (trainee nods). I heard someone call it e-nag, that's pretty clever, isn't it? As soon as you get to work, you've got to get straight into it: phone never stops ringing. Bloody receptionist is always late. Can't get the staff these days, can you? (trainee smiles) Anyway, I'm working hard at my desk, when the boss wants to see me. I get up and go into his office and sit down. He closes the door behind me, sits down and faces me, then he drops the bombshell – the bastard is transferring me to another department. I was gobsmacked. It just came straight out of the blue.

The client's account of the A before the 'bombshell' is irrelevant: it adds nothing to the trainee's understanding of A. After the bombshell, the information is pertinent and emotionally charged. In order to focus the client's mind on clinically relevant detail about A, the trainee could either intervene earlier or ask the client to summarize the most important aspect of the activating event (Walen et al., 1992):

Trainee: (intervenes during the client's discussion of his emails) Can I stop you there? I don't understand what the problem is with all this detail you're giving me. Is it a work-related problem?

Client: Yes, it is. I was just setting the scene. I'm getting to it.

Trainee: Could you pinpoint the nub of the problem without any more scene setting?

Client: My boss is transferring me to another department. I'm furious about it. It's like a bolt from the blue.

[The client has pinpointed an important A and revealed a C.]

Allowing lengthy descriptions of A may give the misleading impression to your clients that A is all-important, when, in fact, B is the major focus of assessment. Clients will need guidance from you in learning succinctness in describing their As – the first step in the problem-solving process.

Key Point

Encourage your clients to be succinct when describing activating events. Model succinctness for them.

---

26 Accepting client vagueness in describing A

Specificity is a guiding principle in REBT; so you will want clear and precise information from your clients regarding the ABCs of their presenting problems. Some clients will communicate in an imprecise, vague way that appears to describe the problem but actually says nothing much at all. In this dialogue, the trainee does not attempt to dispel the vagueness and replace it with clarity:

Client: It's something about, something around, relationships.

Trainee: So the problem is relationships then; so what is the problem with relationships?

Client: It's that whole intimacy thing, you know what I mean?

Trainee: Right. Intimacy in relationships is the problem.

Client: That's it. Something around that.

Trainee: I think we're getting somewhere. So what goal would you like to achieve?

[Goal setting will be difficult without a clear problem to address.]

'Getting somewhere' is more likely to be getting nowhere as therapy drifts aimlessly. Modelling specificity helps your clients to reply in kind:

Client: It's something about, something around, relationships.

Therapist: 'Something about, something around' doesn't help us to define what the problem is. With relationships, is it forming them, maintaining them or breaking-up?

Client: (concentrating) Well, it's, I suppose, . . . maintaining them.

Therapist: What prevents you from maintaining them?

Client: It's that whole intimacy thing, you know what I mean?

Therapist: Not at the moment. If you can supply me with specific information, that will really help me to understand your difficulties. What is it about intimacy that troubles you?

Client: Well, sort of expressing that other side of yourself to others.

Therapist: Do you mean showing your feelings to others, your sensitive side?

Client: Yes.

Therapist: And, if you do show that side of yourself to others . . . ?

Client: They might take advantage of it, exploit me, hurt me, something like that.

Therapist: And, if they did do those things . . . ?

Client: I'd never forgive myself for putting myself in that position in the first place.

Therapist: So, to sum up then: you avoid intimacy because you believe that, if you show your feelings, then you will be exploited or hurt in some way, and you'd never forgive yourself for putting yourself in such a position for that to happen. Is that correct?

[The therapist could also have asked the client what is the worst aspect of the problem for him: being exploited by others, allowing himself to be intimate and thereby placing himself in a vulnerable position, or the implications of never forgiving himself?]

Client: Yes. I want the intimacy, but I fear it.

[The client's last four replies have avoided vagueness – prompted by the therapist's quest for clarity about the A. The therapist then moves on to elicit a C (already indicated by the client's fear of intimacy) and a specific example of the target problem.]

Key Point

Seek and model precision in eliciting information about your clients' As.

27 Allowing clients to talk compulsively about their feelings

REBT seeks to discover and challenge the irrational ideas behind clients' disturbed feelings, not focus excessively on the disturbed feelings themselves. Ellis suggests that 'many clients, some of them trained to do so by previous therapy, long-windedly and compulsively talk about their feelings, their feelings, their feelings' (1991: 6). You might believe indulging clients in endless 'feeling talk' will ameliorate their emotional problems. However, REBT is a cognitive theory of emotional disorders: emotional amelioration occurs through quickly locating, challenging and changing disturbance-inducing ideas. Ironically, ventilation of feelings is

> a highly cognitive activity in which irrational ideas that give rise to strong emotional reactions are rehashed. Giving vent to feelings thus serves to further habituate the ideas that cause the disturbance so that, in effect, the client actually practices being disturbed. As a result, s/he gets worse rather than better (Grieger and Boyd, 1980: 118).

In the following extract, the trainee listens passively (see Point 8) while the client expatiates on her feelings, instead of intervening to help the client make ABC sense of them:

Client: I feel that things just don't work out for me. Why me all the time? My relationship was going so well until I told him that I loved him and that was the end of that. He left, walked out, never returned. Why did he do that to me when all I said was I loved him? I was so devastated by his response, incredibly hurt and angry. I felt everything was out of control in my life. I just felt completely dead inside. What did I do to deserve this, to be treated like this? There's something wrong with me: I must be defective in some way. Why did he dump me? What did I do wrong?

[These 'feelings' are actually a collection of As, Bs and Cs.]

Trainee: So the unexpected end of the relationship came as a devastating blow? That must have been really hard to take.

[The trainee's response, while empathic, could also have directed the client's attention to making explicit some of the irrational ideas behind her 'feeling talk' (e.g. 'I must be defective in some way' – what would be the precise form of her self-deprecation?). Unfortunately, such a response encourages further ventilation of feelings.]

Client: Absolutely. I can't focus, sleep . . . (the client continues in this vein for the rest of the session).

In this dialogue, after the client's initial outpouring, the therapist steps in to put together an ABC picture from the jumble of data presented by the distraught client:

Therapist: Now, is the event, or A, being dumped by your boyfriend when you told him you loved him?

Client: Yes. I was devastated.

Therapist: Now, at C, or emotional consequences, you said you felt angry and hurt. Does devastated refer to one or other of those emotions or something else?

Client: I think depressed, but I was angry, hurt, depressed, all of it.

Therapist: Which feeling shall we focus on first?

Client: I don't know.

Therapist: A lot of your thinking, such as 'What did I do to deserve this, to be treated like this?', refers to feeling hurt. Shall we start there?

Client: Okay. I do feel very hurt. He shouldn't have done this to me. I shouldn't be treated like this after everything I've done for him.

[The implied 'shoulds' in the client's rhetorical questions, which are in all probability absolute, have now been made explicit by her.]

Therapist: You've just supplied two beliefs that we can begin to examine to see whether they are helping or hindering your adjustment to this painful situation. But let me teach you the REBT view of things first.

Key Point

Teach your clients that emotional change is derived from cognitive change, not compulsive or excessive discussion of their feelings.

28 Not obtaining a problem list

Clients do not usually present with one clear, discrete problem. More likely, a number of problem areas will emerge, which may encourage some clients to feel that they are overwhelmed with problems. The importance of a problem list is stated by Fennell:

> Drawing up an agreed problem-list gives the patient immediate experience of cognitive behaviour therapy as a collaborative enterprise. It helps the therapist to understand the patient's perspective, and allows patients to feel that a genuine effort is being made to grasp their internal reality . . . [T]he problem-list also imposes order on chaos. A mass of distressing experiences is reduced to a number of relatively specific difficulties. This process of 'problem-reduction' is crucial to the encouragement of hope, since it implies the possibility of control (1989: 179).

In this excerpt from supervision, the trainee has allowed himself to be sucked into the client's 'chaos':

Supervisor: (listening to session tape) The client obviously has a lot of problems and is jumping from one to the other. Why are you following instead of sticking with one of them?

Trainee: Well, she said that all her problems are equally important, and they're all connected to one another; so how can you just pick out one to look at?

Supervisor: That's her rationale; it doesn't have to be yours too. This jumping around is not going to help her very much. What could you do to bring some stability into therapy?

Trainee: Draw up the problem list I should have done in the first place.

Supervisor: Exactly. Acknowledge they are all connected, but then stick with the chosen problem.

Trainee: What about them all being equally important?

Supervisor: They may be all equally important, but they cannot all be equally examined at the same time. Get this point across to her. Then you, or she, select one problem from the list to explore. Okay?

Trainee: Okay. It does make sense to do it that way.

Key Point

Draw up a problem list with your client and explain the rationale for it.

---

29 Not asking for a specific example of the target problem

A target problem is better understood through specific examples of its occurrence – these examples put flesh on the bones of the target problem. These specific examples are more likely to provide you with accurate information about clients' thoughts, feelings and behaviours than a general or abstract discussion of the target problem. The client's level of emotional engagement with the problem is usually higher at the specific level than the general level. In the following dialogue, the trainee maroons the target problem at the general level:

Trainee: What problem would you like to start with?

Client: I'm anxious a lot of the time. Can't seem to relax, on edge. That sort of thing. It's not nice to feel like that. You see other people having a laugh, enjoying themselves and you think, 'Why can't I be like them?'

Trainee: So you're anxious a lot of the time. So what do you think is going on?

Client: What do you mean?

Trainee: Why do you think you're anxious a lot of the time?

Client: I don't know. I just am.

Trainee: Tell me some more about the anxiety then.

With this approach, the trainee is unlikely to become knowledgeable about the cognitive determinants of the client's anxiety. In the next dialogue, the therapist encourages the client to root his anxiety in concrete contexts:

Therapist: You said that you are anxious a lot of the time. Can you give me a recent or typical example of when you are anxious?

Client: Not really. I'm anxious most of the time, as I said.

Therapist: Okay. Are you anxious right now?

Client: Yes.

Therapist: What thoughts are going through your mind (tapping forehead) at this very moment to make you anxious?

Client: You'll think I'm pathetic because I can't sort out my own problems.

Therapist: And, if I do think that . . . ?

Client: Then you'll reject me, won't want to see me again.

Therapist: And, if I did reject you because I saw you as pathetic, then what?

Client: That's it. Another person not bothering with me because I'm pathetic.

[The client is hinting at the possible cross-situational nature of the problem. See Point 36 for a discussion of moving from a specific to a general understanding of a client's problem. However, when you are assessing a specific example, do not let your clinical focus shift to the general level.]

Therapist: So, to sum up: what you are most anxious about at this moment is that I will be another person in your life who will see you as pathetic and reject you, and you will agree with this view of yourself. Is that correct?

Client: That's it in a nutshell. Shall I leave now?

If you find it difficult to locate or work with a specific example of your client's target problem, you might find the following points helpful. A specific example occurs at a specific time in a specific place and with specific people present (if relevant). By making the example as concrete as possible, a video- or audiotape recording could be made of it (imagine trying to make a recording of a general example).

Key Point

Always ask your client for a specific example(s) of the target problem. Make the details of the example as clear as possible.

30 Readily assuming that an irrational belief is the client's problem

In your haste to find the must and its derivatives, you may pay little attention to actually understanding the client's problem from his viewpoint as you assume his problem is irrational thinking. Trainees

> fall into the trap of confusing the dependent variable (the client's problem) with the therapist's constructs hypothesized to be maintaining the problem (e.g., need for approval, low frustration tolerance). As a result they uncritically accept the notion that the problem is the hypothetical construct (e.g., need for approval or low frustration tolerance). However, irrational beliefs and dysfunctional schemas are not the client's problem. They are the clinician's hypothetical construct of what he or she believes to be the mediating variable that influences the problem (Beal and DiGiuseppe, 1998: 133).

In this excerpt, the trainee wastes no time in pinning a diagnosis on the client:

Client: I hate being held up in traffic jams, queues, that sort of thing, because I like to be punctual, create a good impression.

Trainee: You've got low frustration tolerance.

Client: Have I? Maybe.

Careful assessment is needed before identifying the hypothesized mediating variable:

Therapist: Which do you hate more: being delayed in some way or not being punctual, not creating a good impression?

Client: Being late, not creating a good impression.

Therapist: What does it mean to you, if you don't create a good impression?

Client: I think people, my colleagues, will lose their respect for you.

Therapist: And, if you did lose their respect . . . ?

Client: I would lose respect for myself. It's very important not to lose their respect.

Therapist: What would you be telling yourself to lose respect for yourself?

Client: Well, something like 'If they think I'm incompetent, then that means I am'.

Therapist: So would you say that you absolutely have to have their respect, and, if you don't have it, then you will engage in self-depreciation?

Client: That seems like an accurate summary of the problem. Yes, I'll go along with that.

[The hypothesized mediating variable, a need for others' respect, has been confirmed by the client.]

Key Point

Do not assume that your hypothesis is the client's problem. Your hypothesis needs to be confirmed or disconfirmed by careful assessment of the client's problem.

31 Failing to intervene to make imprecise emotional Cs precise

REBT is primarily focused on emotional problem solving, i.e. disturbed or unhealthy negative emotions (e.g. depression, guilt, shame, hurt and anger). When clients are asked about how they feel in response to adverse life events, they will often reply with such terms as 'stressed-out', 'bad', 'fucked-up' and 'upset'. Which unhealthy negative emotions do these terms refer to? This needs to be clarified before an examination of the emotion begins. Some trainees take these vague descriptions of C on trust – that in a general sense they indicate disturbed feelings:

Trainee: What are you upset about?

Client: I'm upset when I miss my deadlines at work.

[The upset could be a healthy negative emotion like annoyance. If this is the case and the trainee does not pick it up, then the client may be taught that all negative feelings are unhealthy.]

Trainee: What's upsetting about it?

Client: I get really pissed off when I miss it.

[Another vague description of C . . .]

Trainee: What are you pissed off about?

[. . . which the trainee again does not seek to clarify.]

The quickest way to establish the presence of an unhealthy negative emotion is to spell out what you are looking for: 'When you say "upset", do you mean anger, anxiety or hurt, for example?' This can begin clients' education about unhealthy negative emotions. Another vague description of C is through the use of inferences:

Trainee: How do you feel about not being invited to the party?

71

Client: (emphatically) I felt rejected by my friends.

['Rejected' is an inference, not an emotion, which the trainee should point out and then ask: 'How do you feel when you believe you have been rejected?']

Trainee: It sounds like you feel pretty strongly about that?

Client: I damn well do. I feel betrayed by them.

[The client does feel strongly, but what is the feeling? She provides another inference – 'betrayed'. The trainee could have asked forcefully 'How do you feel in your gut about being betrayed by them?' as a way of focusing the client's attention on her emotions.]

Another vague description of C is an extended or lengthy statement about A:

Trainee: How do you feel about being passed over for promotion?

Client: I feel it is an outrage after my years of loyal service to the company. I have an exemplary sickness record, consistently excellent evaluation reports. I gave my heart and soul for that company, and what did they give me in return? The shaft. Why did I break my back for all those years when this is how they treat me?

Trainee: Right . . . hmm . . . well . . . er . . . and how do you feel about that?

[The trainee is overwhelmed by the client's reply and struggles to formulate her own response. Her question is to provide her with time to collect her thoughts rather than pinpoint an unhealthy negative emotion.]

If the trainee had been listening attentively, she could have pointed out to the client:

Trainee: That's a very powerful description of what you have given to the company and how, from your viewpoint, they have behaved in return. You may have suggested how you feel with the term 'outrage' but explicitly, what is the emotion in your gut about getting 'the shaft'?

Client: Unbelievably fucking angry!

Key Point

Ensure that you help your clients to be precise in labelling their disturbed feelings.

32 Not explaining why disturbed feelings are unhealthy/unhelpful and non-disturbed feelings are healthy/helpful

REBT makes the important distinction between unhealthy and healthy negative emotions (e.g. anxiety vs. concern respectively). While it can be difficult for clients to see clearly the differences between these emotional states, nevertheless

> the distinction between disturbed and nondisturbed C's can serve to give a clear focus to one of the main goals in therapy: transforming suffering into appropriate, adaptive, albeit negative emotions (Walen et al., 1992: 92).

Some trainees believe that just by labelling emotions as healthy or unhealthy this 'transformation of suffering' will occur:

Client: Those bastards next door to me play loud music all the time. They are driving me round the bend. I get so angry, I could put my fist through the wall!

Trainee: That loud music must be hard to take, but your angry response is unhealthy.

Client: What do you mean unhealthy? It's perfectly healthy and justified. You try living next door to those bastards.

Trainee: In REBT, we call anger an unhealthy negative emotion. So, if you stopped feeling angry, then you could develop a healthy negative emotion, like annoyance.

[Whether the client feels angry or annoyed, the noise from next door still needs to be addressed.]

Client: Do you mean just feel annoyed about it? What are you going on about? I'm getting angry with this conversation: you don't seem to be listening to me!

73

The client gets angrier while the trainee spouts REBT jargon. Anger can be particularly difficult for clients to surrender as they often feel justified in its expression and giving it up can mean becoming a 'wimp'. Terjesen et al. suggest that 'successful anger treatment usually entails exploration of the consequences of the client's emotions, and the generation of new alternative reactions. These maneuvers motivate the client to change' (1997: 159):

Therapist: I'm sure it's dreadful living with that loud music from next door, but has your anger made any impact on reducing the noise levels?

Client: What do you mean?

Therapist: Have you repeatedly asked them to turn it down?

Client: I did once, but I fear that, if I get my hands on them, I'll do them serious violence.

Therapist: By only asking once, do you think you are showing them how important this issue is for you?

Client: Probably not.

Therapist: Have you contacted the local council about the noise? They are pretty tough on that subject.

Client: No. I didn't think of that.

Therapist: Or the police, if you are really desperate?

Client: Nor them. You make me seem all anger but no action.

Therapist: The bottom line is this: is your anger delivering the goods?

Client: No, it isn't. If I'm not angry, am I supposed to just stand there and take it?

Therapist: You've been 'taking it' for some time now without any results. You could learn to be assertive with your neighbours instead of angry with them. How do you think you would feel, if you acted assertively instead of angrily?

Client: Well, I'd feel determined to do something more useful about their noise, like some of the things you suggested.

Therapist: When you say determined, what feeling does that relate to?

Client: I don't know. Just determined, that's all.

[The therapist does not want to appear to be pedantic in trying to label the feeling at this point in therapy, but she will monitor the client's behaviour to determine whether 'I'd feel determined' is an undisturbed or disturbed emotion.]

Therapist: So, does feeling determined mean you can start working on an action plan: being focused instead of explosive?

Client: It does mean that. Action will be much better than impotent rage. I'm sure it's putting a great strain on my heart.

Therapist: So, let me help you to get over your unhealthy anger so you can take productive action.

When your clients acknowledge that their disturbed emotions are unhealthy, do not assume that their emotional goal is to change them for healthy or non-disturbed feelings. If some clients are reluctant or ambivalent about this proposed emotional shift, undertake a cost-benefit analysis of keeping, vs. changing, the disturbed feelings.

Key Point

Take time to explain to your clients what constitutes unhealthy and healthy negative emotions. Encourage your clients to adopt the latter emotions as emotional goals.

33 Not exploring your clients' reactions to experiencing healthy negative emotions

Healthy negative emotions like remorse or sorrow may not appear healthy to all of your clients. Some clients may have, from the REBT viewpoint, unhealthy negative emotions about these healthy negative emotions. This point can slip your attention if you only listen for the 'healthiness' of the healthy negative emotion:

Client: I felt annoyed about not getting the promotion.

Trainee: Isn't that a healthy response to not getting what you want?

Client: I suppose so.

[The client has some doubts about this.]

Trainee: Now, if you were really angry or in a rage about losing the promotion, that would be something for us to discuss, right?

Client: I suppose so.

[The client has not been reassured.]

In your eagerness to convince clients about the benefits or appropriateness of experiencing healthy negative emotions, you may not be paying attention to clues from them (as in the above dialogue) that they do not agree with your viewpoint:

Therapist: When you say 'I suppose so', that usually means a person has reservations. Do you have reservations about the healthiness of annoyance with regard to not getting the promotion?

Client: I shouldn't have felt anything. I like to take setbacks in my stride.

Therapist: But, as you felt annoyed, you didn't take this setback in your stride, what does that mean about you?

Client: That I'm weak.

Therapist: And how do feel when you see yourself as 'weak'?

Client: (voice drops) Ashamed.

[Ironically, the client is creating more emotional problems for himself by seeing healthy negative emotions as a sign of weakness; accepting these healthy feelings would probably have resulted in fewer problems for him.]

The client's feelings of shame now become the focus of clinical examination (see Point 50 for a discussion of meta-emotional problems). Some clients may view calmness as a healthy emotional response to unpleasant events, which you may agree with. However, calmness may be a self-defeating strategy:

Therapist: You say you want to feel calm about your girlfriend leaving you. Calmness implies you don't care about the end of the relationship. Is that true?

Client: No, I do care.

Therapist: If you do care, then that suggests you do feel something rather than being calm about it. What would be the problem about feeling sad, for example, about the end of the relationship?

Client: I suppose all that emotional hassle I'd go through wanting her back but knowing she isn't coming back.

Therapist: But by trying to avoid that 'emotional hassle', aren't you attempting to deny or suppress your rational desires for the relationship not to have ended?

Client: You mean like living a lie?

Therapist: Yes. Feeling sad, for example, helps you to acknowledge honestly the loss of the relationship, express your feelings about it and constructively adapt to the loss. Whereas pretending you're indifferent about it . . .

Client: Creates the illusion I'm coping with it, when, in reality, I'm not. To be honest, I'm not indifferent to it at all.

[The client is now receptive to an exploration of how he genuinely feels about the end of the relationship.]

Key Point

Remember to explore your clients' idiosyncratic reactions to experiencing healthy negative emotions.

34 Pressurizing clients to be exact about their feelings

Though you are expected to collect precise information from clients regarding their emotional Cs, this collection should not be conducted as though you are giving your clients the third degree:

Trainee: How do you feel when you know you are going to be late for a meeting?

Client: I'm not sure, a feeling of dread usually comes over me.

Trainee: (sharply) When you say 'dread', do you mean 'anxious'?

Client: It's difficult to say. It's an unpleasant feeling.

Trainee: (impatiently) It might be unpleasant, but is it anxiety you're feeling?

You can get into this impatient state if you expect clients to deliver answers as though they were reading from an REBT textbook or believe that clients have ready access to their feelings and are able to label them in an REBT-approved way. Treat your impatience as an A and ask yourself how you feel about it at C. If you are angry, for example, this might reflect low frustration tolerance: 'Clients must give me the right answers to my questions straightaway. When they don't, I can't stand the work I have to do to get the right answers.' Helping clients to be exact about their feelings usually requires some investigation:

Therapist: You say it could be a 'feeling of dread', this might refer to anxiety. When people are anxious, they usually fear that something unpleasant or bad is going to happen to them.

Client: I do fear that. If I get to the meetings late, people will see me as undisciplined and not take my views seriously.

Therapist: So, can we call this feeling 'anxiety' for the time being and explore it further?

Client: Okay. What if it isn't, though?

Therapist: Well, as we collect more information about the problem, this will enable us to pinpoint the emotion with greater precision. We certainly don't want to work on an emotion you're not actually feeling.

Client: That sounds fine.

Key Point

Help your clients to pinpoint their disturbed feelings. If they find this difficult to do, watch for your own impatience and, if present, deal with it.

35 Treating frustration as a C instead of an A

Trainees often see frustration as a C as they believe it is synonymous with anger. As a C, frustration is usually viewed by REBT theory as a healthy negative emotion that clients experience when they are blocked from attaining their goals (Dryden et al., 1999). However, when clients state they are feeling frustrated, this could mean they are experiencing an unhealthy negative emotion. This confusion over frustration as a C is discussed by the supervisor:

Supervisor: You are assuming the client's frustration is an unhealthy negative emotion.

Trainee: He's frustrated about his workload piling up.

Supervisor: His frustration could act as a source of motivation to do something constructive about the workload.

Trainee: I didn't think of that. So how do I find out whether his frustration is helpful or not?

Supervisor: Treat his frustration about the workload as an A, then ask him whether it is bearable or unbearable.

Trainee: And, if it's unbearable . . . ?

Supervisor: Then that probably points to a disturbed feeling like anger or anxiety, which you can help him tackle, or it may point to counterproductive behaviours like procrastination or impulsiveness, which also require your clinical attention.

Trainee: And, if it's bearable . . . ?

Supervisor: Then move on to a problem which isn't.

Key Point

Treat your client's frustration as an A in order to determine whether the C is a healthy or unhealthy negative emotion.

36 Generalizing from an emotional C when you need to be specific, and being specific when it is important to generalize

Emotional Cs need to be connected to specific situations in order for accurate assessment information to be collected. This helps clients to see that their disturbed feelings are generated by the beliefs that they hold about these situations, not by the situations themselves (further reinforcing emotional responsibility). This examination of situation-specific feelings is undermined by some trainees' tendency to shift the focus to the general level when they are at the point of entering a specific A:

Trainee: Can you think of a specific example of when you are anxious?

Client: Yes, I can: when I'm asked to give my opinion about something during a meeting.

Trainee: Are there other situations when you feel anxious also?

[The trainee should have analysed the situation she asked the client to provide for her.]

Client: Yes, there are.

Trainee: Why do you think you get anxious?

[This question is best answered after data has been collected, not in the absence of it.]

On the other hand, you might take the client through endless ABC examples (a tunnel-vision approach) without helping him to stand back and see his problems panoramically, i.e. is there a theme running through these situations that points to a core irrational belief (e.g. 'I must have the approval of others. Without it, I'm no good')? In problem assessment, start with understanding the client's emotional C in specific contexts before attempting generalizations about it.

Key Point

Remember that your clinical focus is required at both specific and general levels of assessment; so learn when to switch your focus to help your clients understand their problems in greater depth.

---

37 Focusing on a behavioural C instead of using it to find an emotional C

In the ABC model, C also stands for behavioural consequences. However, REBT is primarily concerned with finding and ameliorating disturbed emotional Cs (e.g. depression). Behavioural Cs provide useful information about what the emotional C might be. In this dialogue, the trainee is just discussing the client's behaviour instead of using it to deduce the emotional C:

Client: When he's upset me, I just won't talk to him for days. I sleep in the spare room. I try to avoid bumping into him around the house.

Trainee: That must be difficult.

Client: It's hard to avoid each other and it's stupid behaviour looking back on it, but at the time I can't bear to be near him when he's upset me like that.

Trainee: What do you do with yourself when you can't bear to be near him?

[The trainee should be looking for behavioural clues, like 'sulking', which indicate the presence of hurt – the most likely emotional C in this case, which, of course, needs to be confirmed by the client.]

A particularly difficult behavioural C to assess is procrastination. Procrastination is often a behavioural means of protecting individuals from experiencing disturbed feelings if they engaged in the avoided activity. A common mistake among trainees is to focus on the emotional consequences of procrastination (e.g. guilt, anger, shame) as though these were the key emotional Cs to examine, when, in fact, the key ones are 'hidden' by the procrastination. In this excerpt, the therapist does not make this mistake:

Therapist: I understand why you are angry with yourself for not getting on with the task, but it is important to find out what prevents you from getting on with it.

Client: I don't know what it is.

Therapist: Okay. Now really imagine getting down to the task, not avoiding it. How are you feeling?

Client: Pretty good.

[Clients often feel positive when they imagine themselves tackling their procrastination; so why are they depriving themselves of this feeling by not getting on with it?]

Therapist: That feeling might come when you get into the task, but how might you feel at the beginning of the task?

Client: Uncomfortable.

Therapist: Would that mean anxious?

[The therapist assesses whether 'uncomfortable' is an unhealthy negative emotion.]

Client: Yes. I'm feeling tense now.

Therapist: What would you be anxious about?

Client: That my report might not be up to the high standards my boss demands.

Therapist: And, if your report fell below these high standards . . . ?

Client: Then I'd be seen as the incompetent in the team. I do not want that label attached to me.

Therapist: So does the procrastination help you to avoid this feared outcome?

Client: At the moment it does, but not for much longer if I miss the deadline for the report.

Therapist: Well, let's find ways to tackle your anxiety about being 'seen as the incompetent in the team' if the report falls below your boss's high standards.

If clients are unable to identify in the session the 'hidden' emotion under-pinning their procrastination, then ask them to engage in the avoided activity outside of the session in order to uncover it. When counterproduct-ive behavioural Cs (e.g. excessive alcohol consumption) are initiated to avoid experiencing disturbed feelings, encourage your clients to stop the counterproductive behaviour (e.g. cease drinking) and tackle construct-ively the disturbed feelings that are no longer being 'drowned by the booze'.

An important point to remember is that counterproductive behavioural Cs can exist in their own right, i.e. they are neither tied to disturbed feelings nor 'hide' them. When this is the case, they are treated as C in an ABC episode and the episode is assessed in the usual way. Behavioural problem solving demonstrates the flexibility of REBT in action: namely, that you do not need to elicit a disturbed emotion from your client before therapy can proceed.

Key Point

Explore behavioural Cs in order to uncover emotional Cs, but there will be occasions when behavioural Cs exist in their own right and are tackled that way.

38 Becoming obsessive in searching for the critical A

When you are assessing the A, the specific example of the client's target problem, it is important to find the aspect of the A which triggered your client's irrational beliefs and thereby explains the presence of the C that you have already elicited. This aspect of the A is called the 'critical A' and can be seen as the emotionally hottest part of the A or that part of it which your client pays most attention to. A very effective way of locating the critical A is through inference chaining, i.e. inferences your client makes about the A are often chained together, and it is your task to help the client identify the particular inference in the chain that functions as the trigger for the irrational belief.

While locating the critical A can be a straightforward task, inference chaining is usually required if the A is not readily apparent or there is a number of competing As the client is disturbed about. Trainees often become obsessed with uncovering the critical A for the following reasons: to prove their competence as REBT therapists, they get carried away with the intellectual challenge and excitement of tracking it down or erroneously believe that the critical A is always the last inference in the chain and so keep pushing the chain as far as it will go (the critical A can be found *anywhere* in the chain; see Point 40). Unfortunately, as well as wasting valuable therapy time, you can exhaust the patience of your clients:

Trainee: What's anxiety provoking in your mind about moving in with your girlfriend?

Client: That means I've made a commitment to her.

Trainee: And, if you have a commitment to her, then what?

Client: Then I'll have to prove myself to her.

Trainee: In what specific way or ways have you got to prove yourself to her?

[The trainee seeks clarification of 'got to prove myself to her' before attempting to continue inference chaining.]

Client: Lots of things: stop screwing around, hold down a job, be acceptable to her parents, be a good stepfather to her daughter, not appear stupid in front of her posh friends, give up drinking, mend my bad ways. Things like that.

Trainee: Which one of those things are you most anxious about?

Client: I'm anxious about all of them.

Trainee: Isn't there one that's more anxiety provoking for you than the others, like holding down a job for example?

Client: It's hard to say. I've never had a good work record.

Trainee: So is that it then: holding down a job?

Client: That would worry me, yes. But, if I didn't give up drinking, that would worry me too. It's hard to say which one would give me the most grief.

Trainee: But one of them must cause you greater anxiety than the rest.

[In his determination to find the critical A, the trainee does not notice he has slipped into A–C language.]

Client: (irritated) I don't know what to say to you other than I don't know which one!

Trainee: Therapy can't proceed until we've found the critical A; so we have to keep looking for it.

[This is untrue. Therapy can proceed if the trainee undisturbs himself about finding the critical A. The rest of the session is taken up with a fruitless search for it, thereby putting the therapeutic relationship under considerable strain.]

Finding the critical A can be an exceedingly difficult task at times (see Neenan and Dryden, 1999), and determining what the critical A is can change from session to session as more information is uncovered to refine it even further (do not see a revealed critical A as definitive). As trainees, find a reasonably important A that you can work on with your client, elicit the irrational beliefs the client has about this A and then show him how to dispute these beliefs. Teaching your client the ABCDE sequence of an emotional episode gets therapy moving quickly, instead of it stalling because of your obsessive search for the critical A. Also, once your clients start thinking in REBT ways, they often initiate their own search for the critical A in each emotional episode examined. In this dialogue, the therapist settles for pinpointing a reasonable A to examine:

Therapist: You mentioned a number of things you believe you'll have to prove to your girlfriend, if you move in with her. Which one of those are you reasonably anxious about?

Client: Being a good stepfather to her daughter.

Therapist: What are you anxious about with regard to that?

Client: That I won't be a stable and reliable father figure.

Therapist: And, if you're not such a figure to her daughter . . . ?

Client: Then I'll be a failure.

[The therapist helps the client to construct his irrational belief about this A: 'I must be a stable and reliable father figure for my girlfriend's daughter because, if I'm not, this will prove I'm a failure.' Disputing can now begin.]

Key Point

Finding the critical A is not critical. Find a reasonably important A to work on to get therapy moving, not stuck.

39 Challenging inferences instead of waiting to dispute uncovered irrational beliefs

When you are inference chaining, it is important to regard each inference uncovered as temporarily true, even if it is grossly distorted. Not challenging the client's inferences allows the chain to unfold until the inference that triggers her irrational belief is revealed. Challenging inferences is likely to stop the inference-chaining process in its tracks, put your client on the defensive and convey to him that inferences are crucial instead of peripheral to his emotional problems:

Trainee: What are you angry about when your wife comes home late from work?

Client: I think she's having an affair.

Trainee: Do you have any evidence for this assumption?

[The next question should have been: 'And, if she is . . . ?']

Client: What do you mean 'evidence'? I have my suspicions, and that's good enough for me. I'm her husband, not you.

Trainee: These suspicions are creating your anger. What you need is hard evidence that she's having an affair instead of jumping to conclusions. Coming home late could have a perfectly innocent explanation, couldn't it?

[The trainee is making an A–C connection by saying 'these suspicions are creating your anger', whereas it is the client's demand about these suspicions that is anger-producing: 'I must know whether my suspicions are accurate. I can't stand the agony of not knowing.' This demand is unlikely to be revealed as the trainee has nominated inferences as the primary cognitive determinant in emotional disturbance.]

Client: Possibly.

Trainee: Why don't you speak to her about your suspicions and see what happens?

Client: (not convinced) I'll think about it.

[The personal significance for the client of his wife's putative infidelity has not been explored, thereby leaving intact his disturbance-producing ideas and no coping strategy in place if his suspicions prove accurate.]

Inferences, which are derived from irrational beliefs, can be challenged *after* some headway has been made in disputing the client's irrational belief (e.g. 'My wife must not be having an affair. If she is, that will be awful'). The validity of the client's inferences usually appears less defensible to him after this disputing process.

Key Point

Only elicit inferences at this stage; do not dispute them.

---

40 Pursuing theoretical inferences instead of clinically significant ones

If you keep on asking, without pause for reflection or review of the unfolding inference chain, 'Let's assume that's true, then what?' questions, do not be surprised when the chain ends with your clients imagining themselves destitute (the novelist, Martin Amis, calls this fear of losing everything 'tramp dread'). Because of your unreflective questioning, the client is providing you with theoretical inferences (i.e. grim events that could occur, but the client is not worried about them) instead of attempting to locate clinically significant inferences (i.e. what the client is actually worried about). In this dialogue, the trainee is oblivious to clues that he is in the realm of theoretical inferences:

Trainee: What would you be anxious about, if you are not successful in your new career as a stress-management consultant?

Client: (visibly tensing) I'm staking everything on being successful.

['Staking everything' needs to be clarified.]

Trainee: But, if you're not successful, then what?

Client: Then I won't get the work?

Trainee: And, if you don't get the work . . . ?

Client: Er . . . hmm . . . er . . . I won't be able to pay the mortgage?

[The client's elongated pauses suggest a lack of affect, and that he is manufacturing an answer. Also, his answer is phrased in the form of a question, which indicates the presence of theoretical inferences, because he is speculating about future outcomes rather than convinced that they will occur.]

Trainee: And, if you can't pay the mortgage . . . ?

Client: Lose the house, I suppose. I don't know.

[The client is perplexed by the trainee's questions.]

Trainee: And, if you lose the house . . . ?

Client: Er . . . end up on the streets? Kill myself? I don't know.

[There is an incongruity between the increasing grimness of the client's inferences and the lack of any corresponding strong affect on his part. He is clearly uninterested in where the trainee is taking the chain.]

Trainee: What are you most anxious about: ending up on the streets or killing yourself?

Client: (becoming irritated with the trainee) Look, I really don't know. What is the point of all this?

When you are teasing out an inference chain, it is important to pay attention to verbal, paraverbal, behavioural and affective clues, which indicate you are on the right road to the critical A, veering away from it or are completely lost. In the above dialogue, the client was visibly tensing at one point, but a few moments later he is displaying no affect. The therapist takes note of this:

Therapist: I think I'm racing ahead of myself: you said, 'I'm staking everything on being successful.' What do you mean by that?

Client: (becoming agitated) If I don't make it in my new career, then I will have been deceiving myself about having good judgement in making this career move.

Therapist: And, if your judgement turns out to be flawed . . . ?

Client: (eyes moistening, voice dropping) Then my faith in my judgement, worse, myself, my faith in myself, will be destroyed.

Therapist: Is that what you are most anxious about: that if you are unsuccessful in your new career, your faith in yourself will be destroyed?

Client: (staring at the floor) Yes. That's what I fear the most.

[The client's actual fears have been uncovered. Notice the differences between the client's present emotional state and how he was when theoretical inferences were being assessed.]

Key Point

Pay careful attention to the clues offered by your clients that indicate you might be eliciting theoretical inferences instead of clinically relevant ones.

41 Not realizing that your client's target emotion has changed

When conducting inference chaining, it is important to keep your client's target emotion as the driving force behind the clinical enquiry (e.g. 'What is anger-provoking in your mind . . . ?') in order to locate the critical A. However, clients will not always give you inferences associated with the 'driving force' emotion, but ones that suggest the target emotion has changed. In this dialogue, the trainee does not detect an emotional shift:

Trainee: What would you be anxious about in the group?

Client: I might not be able to answer the questions?

Trainee: What would you be anxious about, if you couldn't answer the questions?

Client: I'd be exposed in the group as an idiot. I'd be an object of derision within the group (the client gazes at the floor, avoiding eye contact with the trainee).

[The client's reply suggests that the target emotion has changed: having your perceived defects revealed publicly is usually associated with shame. Also, avoiding eye contact protects the client from the presumed critical scrutiny of others, whether actually or psychologically present. The trainee could have asked the client how she was feeling at that moment.]

Trainee: What would you be anxious about, if you were exposed as an idiot?

Client: Who wants to be exposed as an idiot?

Trainee: Probably no one, but what would you be anxious about, if you were exposed as an idiot?

Client: I wouldn't like it.

This clinical enquiry is proving unproductive as the client is experiencing a different emotion to the one the trainee is still pursuing. It is important to learn the themes tied to particular emotions (see Dryden et al., 1999) in order to detect emotional shifts during inference chaining. Also, a change in your client's target emotion is more likely to occur when the initial target emotion is anxiety. Anxiety involves future-orientated thinking; so when you encourage your client to bring the future into the present (i.e. assume that the future feared event has occurred), the target emotion often changes:

Therapist: What would you be anxious about, if you couldn't answer the questions?

Client: I'd be exposed in the group as an idiot. I'd be an object of derision within the group.

Therapist: Assuming that happened, how would you feel at that point?

Client: I'd be ashamed.

Therapist: You'd feel ashamed because . . . ?

Client: Because they would see me as an idiot.

Therapist: And would you agree with the group's judgement of you as an idiot?

[You cannot be an 'idiot' unless you agree with others' evaluation of you.]

Client: (avoiding eye contact) Yes, I would.

At this point, you can ask your client whether she wants to conduct an ABC analysis of future exposure as an 'idiot' associated with her anxiety or one focused on being exposed as an 'idiot' connected with her shame.

Key Point

Learn the themes associated with particular emotions in order to assist you in detecting emotional shifts during inference chaining. These shifts are more likely to occur when the target emotion is anxiety.

42 Not noticing that your client has provided you with a C instead of an inference

During inference chaining, your clients might provide you with behavioural or emotional Cs in reply to your questions. When this occurs, it is important to ask 'Why' questions to avoid the hunt for the critical A being sidetracked (Moore, 1988) – which is what happens in this excerpt:

Trainee: What were you hurt about when your partner turned up an hour late?

Client: That he takes me for granted.

Trainee: And, if he does take you for granted, then what?

Client: I could smash his face in!

[This seems like anger, a C. The trainee treats it as an inference.]

Trainee: And, if you did smash his face in . . . ?

Client: (matter-of-factly) He would end up in hospital, and I would be charged by the police with assault.

Trainee: And, if you were charged with assault . . . ?

Any emotional tension has gone from the inference chain. The trainee's questions and the client's replies are equally mechanical. The trail of the critical A has gone cold. To get back on the right trail, the trainee should have asked:

Trainee: Why do you want to smash his face in?

Client: Because he knows I love him, and he doesn't return it.

Trainee: And, if he doesn't return it . . . ?

Client: (starts crying) Then my love has been in vain: all for nothing. I've been taken for a fool and that's what hurts the most.

Key Point

Ask 'Why' questions when your clients provide you with Cs during inference chaining.

---

43 Not clarifying the 'it'

When clients use the word 'it' (e.g. 'I can't stand it' or 'It makes me angry'), it is not always clear what the 'it' refers to. When this is the case, you will need to clarify the 'it'. The trainee does not do so in this dialogue:

Trainee: What is anger-provoking in your mind about being turned down, when you asked your colleague, Mary, for a date?

Client: No one wants to get turned down, do they?

Trainee: Probably not, but, as you were turned down . . . ?

Client: I can't stand it.

[This seems like the critical A because the client has articulated an irrational belief. However, does the 'it' refer to being turned down or the consequences of being turned down?]

Trainee: So you can't stand it when Mary turned you down. Let's see whether I can help you stand it.

[The trainee does not explore this question as she believes she has automatically identified the client's critical A because of the presence of the irrational belief.]

An ambiguous 'it' represents an entry point for further exploration of the inference chain, which the therapist now conducts:

Therapist: Can I clarify something with you: does the 'it' just refer to the pain of being turned down?

Client: Well, it does, but I also see her every day at work; so that is very uncomfortable too, working with someone who turned you down.

Therapist: Is there anything else 'I can't stand it' refers to?

Client: The other blokes at work are laughing at me behind my back. They think it's a great laugh that I got the thumbs down. I really fancied her something rotten – still do – and there's no chance of ever going out with her. That really hurts too.

Therapist: The 'it' seems to refer to four things: one, the pain of being turned down; two, feeling very uncomfortable working alongside her; three, the blokes at work laughing at you behind your back; and, four, still really fancying her but knowing there's no chance of ever going out with her. Which one of those four do you believe is the most unbearable?

Client: Definitely number four. I'm thinking of leaving the company so I don't suffer every day when I see her.

[Understanding what the 'it' referred to was not so straightforward after all.]

We might summarize the problem discussed here as: not clarifying the 'it' gets you into the 'shit'!

Key Point

Do not take the 'it' for granted: if there is any hint of ambiguity, explore the 'it'.

44 Using theory-driven questions in assessing irrational beliefs when open-ended questions would be more productive for the client and vice versa

There are two basic ways of assessing clients' irrational beliefs: theory-driven questions and open-ended questions. Theory-driven questions are derived from REBT theory (e.g. 'What *demand* were you making on yourself about passing the exam, which led you to feel anxious?') and 'nudge' the client to provide the answers you are looking for. Open-ended questions, also derived from REBT theory, make the client work harder to pinpoint their demands (e.g. 'What were you telling yourself about passing the exam, which led you to feel anxious?') because you are not providing direct assistance this time (in our experience, clients are likely to provide you with more *inferences* about A than *demands* about A).

By the time you get to assessing irrational beliefs, you have already taught your clients about the role of rigid vs. flexible beliefs in unhealthy and healthy negative emotions respectively (see Point 21) and have identified the A and C elements of your client's presenting problem. But what is the B? Whether theory-driven or open-ended questions are more productive in locating the B depends upon your clients' answers to these questions:

Trainee: What was going through your mind to make you feel angry about not getting the promotion?

[An open-ended question.]

Client: I really wanted it.

[The client expresses a strong preference.]

Trainee: Okay. If you really wanted the promotion but told yourself there is no reason why you *must* get it, would you have still got angry?

[The trainee is indicating that true preferences do not produce emotional disturbance.]

Client: Yes, because one of those bastards on the interview board had it in for me.

[An inference about A.]

Trainee: That's an assumption about why you didn't get the promotion, and we are looking for your evaluation, your summing-up, of not getting the promotion. If I can come back to your strong desire to get the promotion, what do you think you were adding to that strong desire which led to you being so angry when you didn't get the promotion?

Client: I wasn't adding anything – I really wanted to get the promotion. Do you understand that?

[The trainee battles on for the rest of the session even though the client shows no signs of revealing the irrational belief, which is: 'I absolutely should have got the promotion, but, as I didn't get it, the interview board are a bunch of bastards for not giving it to me.']

If your client is struggling to come up with irrational beliefs after several open-ended questions, then consider switching to theory-driven questions to reduce time wasting and possible exasperation on the client's part as he realizes he is not 'saying the right things'. In deciding which method of questioning to use, you should have been assessing from the first session onwards your client's intellectual and verbal abilities to understand and discuss REBT concepts. In this example, the trainee hands the answer to the client when her reply indicates it has been made too easy for her:

Trainee: What demand are you making on yourself about answering questions during the workshop that leads you to feel anxious?

Client: That's easy: I must answer every question perfectly. I remember our earlier discussion of the ABC model and the role of musts and shoulds in producing disturbed feelings like anxiety.

Trainee: You provided excellent feedback on the model. Now, let me ask you another question: what kind of a person do you think you would be, if you don't answer every question perfectly?

[Instead of asking an open-ended question in the light of the client's reply (e.g. 'What would that mean, if you couldn't answer the questions perfectly?'), the trainee continues with the needless strategy of theory-driven questions.]

Client: Again that's easy: I'd see myself as totally incompetent.

Asking theory-driven questions is therapist-led discovery of irrational thinking, while asking open-ended questions encourages self-discovery of such thinking and thereby reduces the risk of you putting words into your client's mouth. A client who takes pride in 'thinking for myself' may object to being 'led by the nose' with theory-driven questions:

Client: You know, I think I can put two and two together myself about the presentation, if it screws up.

Therapist: I apologize for being so obvious in my use of certain questions. So, could you restate what it is you are anxious about?

Client: That I might not give a first-class presentation.

Therapist: . . . and then . . . ?

[The therapist is engaging in conjunctive phrasing, which removes the full stop at the end of the client's sentences and replaces it with a conjunction (e.g. and) to promote further introspection.]

Client: Then the presentation will be crap.

Therapist: . . . and that would mean . . . ?

Client: That would mean I'm crap. That's exactly how I will see myself, if the presentation goes wrong. Now I can hear the demand I'm making without you telling me: 'The presentation must be first class because, if it isn't, that will mean I'm crap.'

[Conjunctive phrasing allowed the client to 'put two and two together myself'.]

Key Point

Deciding which method of questioning to use in assessing irrational beliefs depends on your clients' responses to your questions as well as your own evaluation of their intellectual abilities.

45 Assuming that your clients hold all four irrational beliefs

When you are teaching your clients about 'musturbatory' (musts) thinking and its derivatives as part of your assessment of their irrational beliefs, it can be easy to believe that they hold all four beliefs: the complete set (maybe you have misinterpreted what you have read or what you have been taught). This assumption can mean you are not listening for disconfirming evidence:

Trainee: Now I've explained the role of musts at the core of emotional disturbance and the three irrational beliefs that stem from them. Now let's apply this viewpoint to your problems. Now, what demand are you making about being successful?

Client: I must always be successful. My life story.

Trainee: Now, if you are not always successful, would that be awful, the end of your world?

Client: Well, it wouldn't be very nice, would it?

[The client has not agreed that it would be awful and therefore has not endorsed this irrational belief.]

Trainee: The end of one's personal world isn't usually a nice experience. Would failure be unbearable in terms of low frustration tolerance?

Client: Well, it would be pretty hard to bear.

[The client is implying she could bear it, not that it is unbearable.]

Trainee: Pretty unbearable then. Lastly, do you think you would be putting yourself down in some way, if you weren't always successful?

Client: Absolutely. I would see myself as completely useless, if I failed in any way. I shudder to think about it.

[The client has provided powerful evidence that the must is connected to self-depreciation, not the other two irrational beliefs.]

Trainee: So we've got four irrational beliefs to examine.

Client: Oh dear. It sounds like I've got a lot of problems.

[Only because the trainee was not paying close attention to the client's replies regarding awfulizing and low frustration tolerance.]

Key Point

Do not assume your clients hold all four irrational beliefs: carefully check this out with them.

---

46 Not distinguishing between absolute and preferential shoulds

When you are assessing the premise form of your client's irrational beliefs, she might say for example: 'I should have got straight As in my exams', you assume it is an irrational belief and then move on to assess her derivative belief(s). However, use of the word 'should' does not automatically mean a demand, and you could be disputing a preferential should. In order to distinguish between irrational and rational shoulds, Walen et al. suggest 'it would be wise for the therapist who hears a "should" to rephrase the sentence and feed it back, to ensure that it represents demandingness' (1992: 116).

Therapist: When you say, 'I should have got straight As in my exams', do you mean you absolutely (emphasizes word) should have got them, there is no room in your thinking for accepting that you did not get straight As?

Client: I cannot, will not accept the results. I absolutely should have got top marks in all my subjects.

[The meaning of the client's 'should' is now clear. For a discussion of other non-dogmatic meanings of 'should', see Neenan and Dryden, 1999.]

Key Point

Ensure that you distinguish between irrational and rational shoulds.

---

47 Constructing a general version of the client's situation-specific irrational belief without any evidence for it

Clients can hold irrational beliefs in specific as well as general contexts (e.g. 'I must make you see my viewpoint on this issue' and 'People must understand my viewpoint on all issues that I discuss with them' respectively). When you undertake an ABC analysis of a specific example of your client's target problem, you are more likely to elicit a situation-specific irrational belief than a general belief. In our experience, trainees, without any evidence, often start generalizing from the specific belief:

Client: I know it sounds pathetic, but I do need my wife's approval and, without it, I'm nothing.

[The client's need for approval is only from his wife – the need for approval from others has not been discussed or hinted at.]

Trainee: So, can we say that your irrational belief is: 'I must have the approval of others. Without it, I'm nothing'?

[The trainee is racing ahead of herself by stating what has yet to be established: does the client need the approval of others, and, if he does not get it, would he automatically conclude he was nothing?]

Client: Well . . . hmm . . . I suppose so. I didn't think of it like that, you know, involving others. It might do. I'm just not sure.

Trainee: Having approval needs is a pretty common problem.

[The client is unsure whether he needs approval from others but the trainee is seeking to convince him that he does.]

Client: I suppose it is.

[But is it the client's problem?]

Key Point

When you elicit a situation-specific irrational belief, work on that belief until, and only until, further evidence is uncovered that the belief is a specific example of a more general problem.

48 Not expressing self-depreciation in the client's words

People often depreciate themselves when their demands are not met (e.g. the depression-inducing belief, 'As I didn't get the job, which I absolutely should have done, this means I'm a failure'). When people think in this way, it is called 'ego disturbance'. Sometimes it can appear in REBT that ego disturbance is defined scatologically: 'self-esteem . . . depends on your doing the right thing, and when you do the wrong thing, back to shithood you go . . . shouldhood equals shithood' (Ellis, quoted in Bernard, 1986: 52–3). You might believe that self-depreciation is simply clients calling themselves 'shits'. Clients' self-depreciatory epithets (e.g. worthless, useless) are not necessarily synonymous in their minds with 'shithood' and, therefore, you need to be very wary about introducing the term as a matter of course; in fact, only introduce it when clients actually call themselves 'shits'. Much better to use the client's form of self-depreciation as this will keep you alert to the manifold ways ego disturbance is expressed:

Client: That self-help book you lent me upset me because it says people call themselves 'shits' when things go wrong. I don't call myself that. I was quite offended.

Therapist: I think the book was making a general point. It is much better and more accurate to locate the precise words people use when they put themselves down. What would you call yourself for starting drinking again?

[The therapist does not get sidetracked by the client's A–C thinking – what he read in the book upset him – and focuses on eliciting his idiosyncratic expression of self-depreciation.]

Client: I'm a fraud. I promised myself and others that I would never drink again and here I am, back in therapy.

We have noticed that some trainees use a strange formulation for stating a client's irrational belief involving self-depreciation. For example, they establish the premise part of the belief such as 'I musn't make mistakes' and then add: 'and when you do make them, you put yourself down in some way'. Ensure that you express the self-depreciation belief as clearly as the premise part of the belief.

Key Point

Let your clients describe self-depreciation in their own ways. Do not force 'shithood' on them.

---

49 Not clearly determining whether ego or discomfort disturbance is the primary problem

REBT posits two types of emotional disturbance underlying most, if not all, neurotic problems: ego and discomfort. Ego disturbance involves self-depreciation, while discomfort disturbance views prevailing life conditions as unendurable. While ego and discomfort disturbance are seen as discrete categories, they frequently interact. Therefore, you are advised to be alert to problems in both these areas and when they interact; careful assessment is required to disentangle one from the other. Often, trainees will too readily assume, for example, that avoidance of an onerous task involves discomfort disturbance:

Client: It's going to be a major hassle getting on with the essay when so many parties beckon.

Trainee: What do you think you're telling yourself to stop yourself from getting on with it?

Client: I can't bear the thought of all that research I've got to do.

Trainee: Your attitude to the work reflects what we call in REBT 'low frustration tolerance' or LFT. It sometimes is also called 'I-can't-stand-it-itis'.

Client: (smiles) That sure sounds like me.

While 'procrastination almost always involves LFT' (Wessler and Wessler, 1980: 104), it does not mean that LFT is always the primary disturbance underpinning procrastination as the therapist discovers:

Therapist: If I was able to help you face the 'major hassle' of the research for the essay, would you then be able to get on with it?

Client: If I started on the essay, that would bring up another worry: I might not get a high mark.

Therapist: What would that mean to you, if you didn't get a high mark?

Client: I'd be a failure, big time.

Therapist: So which problem is the greater obstacle for starting the essay: the LFT or seeing yourself as a failure when you don't get a high mark?

Client: The failure part. I get a tight stomach just thinking about it.

[Ego disturbance is the primary problem: 'I must get a high mark, because, if I don't, this will prove I'm a complete failure.']

On the other hand, what seems an obvious case of ego disturbance may not be:

Trainee: What are you anxious about with regard to that talk in a few weeks' time?

Client: Who wants to make a fool of themselves? I'm sure there'll be some questions I can't answer and gaps in my knowledge will be exposed. I'll have to do a lot of preparatory reading to try and avoid that happening. I might actually cancel the talk.

Trainee: So, if these things occur, then you'll see yourself as a fool and that's why you're thinking about cancelling the talk. Is that right?

Client: Yes, that's right.

At first blush, it seems like a case of ego anxiety about making a fool of himself, but the client did refer to having to do a lot of 'preparatory reading' for the talk:

Therapist: Won't the preparatory reading increase the probability of answering all the questions and plugging gaps in your knowledge and thereby reducing the chances of you looking like a fool?

Client: Probably, but reducing the chances of looking like fool means a hell of a lot of work in the next few weeks, a hell of a lot. It will do my head in.

Therapist: Can I just clarify something with you: what are you most anxious about – the preparatory reading or looking like a fool?

Client: All that preparatory stuff. I really cannot be bothered to do it.

Therapist: And is that the real reason you're thinking about cancelling the talk?

Client: You've caught me out, haven't you?

[Discomfort disturbance is the primary problem: 'I absolutely shouldn't have to work this hard to be knowledgeable for the talk. It's too hard, and I can't stand it!']

When ego and discomfort aspects of the problem appear equally strong, discuss with your client which aspect to work on first. With regard to assessing emotional disturbance, it is important to remember that musts on their own do not give a clue as to whether the client's problem is basically ego or discomfort in nature. Musts plus self-depreciation (especially when this belief is stronger than any LFT beliefs present) point to ego disturbance, while musts plus LFT (with the presence of only weak self-depreciation beliefs) suggest discomfort disturbance. Musts plus awfulizing beliefs offer no guide to pinpointing a client's problems as mainly ego or discomfort related. Assess the awfulizing belief to determine this. For example, a client says the end of his marriage is awful: does this refer to seeing himself as a failure or living alone will be unbearable? The client focuses on seeing himself as a 'failure', which indicates that awfulizing is mainly associated with ego disturbance.

One final point: we have recently made a case for the term 'non-ego disturbance' to replace LFT and discomfort disturbance as the generic alternative to ego disturbance in REBT theory (Neenan and Dryden, 1999). The reasons for proposing this new term are outside the scope of this book, but you might be interested in considering them.

Key Point

Go beyond prima facie evidence of your clients' ego or discomfort disturbance to assess carefully whether your initial impressions are correct.

50 Not looking for a meta-emotional problem

One of the unique features of REBT is its emphasis on meta-emotional disturbances or, what some other REBT therapists refer to as, secondary emotional disturbances (Ellis and Bernard, 1985); in other words, our ability to disturb ourselves about our primary emotional disturbances, e.g. angry about feeling anxious or ashamed of feeling jealous. Meta-emotional interference can hinder the client's progress in therapy, e.g. you are tackling the client's jealousy, while he is angry with himself for feeling jealous – there is no agreed emotional-problem focus to work on. In this dialogue excerpt, the trainee is oblivious to the presence of a meta-emotional problem because he is not on the alert for one:

Trainee: Can we examine some recent and specific examples of when you have these angry outbursts? That's how we start off in REBT.

Client: If you want.

Trainee: So, can you provide an example for us to work on?

Client: You know, I shouldn't behave like this. It's wrong to be angry with people who care for you.

[The client is signalling the possible presence of another emotion, which seems to be distracting him from responding to the trainee's questions.]

Trainee: Well, once we start dealing with your anger, then you'll be less likely to behave like that, won't you? So, if we could have an example to work on . . . ?

Client: I think my behaviour is despicable. My wife stood by me through thick and thin, and all she gets is the rough edge of my tongue. I don't deserve her.

Trainee: Is that the example you're giving me?

[The trainee has not picked up that the client's mind is elsewhere.]

Client: Sorry. What?

Two agendas are at work here: the trainee is trying to winkle out of the client a specific example of the target problem, while the client reflects on his 'despicable' behaviour. Unless the trainee detects the meta-emotional problem, therapy will be stalled – an outcome avoided by the therapist in this dialogue:

Therapist: I get the impression that you are distracted in some way, and therefore you are not focused on my questions. Would my assumption be correct? (client nods) Is it to do with your despicable behaviour? (client nods) How do you feel when you think about yourself in this way and the way you've treated your wife?

Client: I feel so guilty. I promise to change my ways, but I don't.

[At this point, client and therapist can decide whether guilt should now replace anger as the focus of clinical attention; see Point 52.]

You can routinely enquire about a meta-emotional problem as soon as your client reveals a primary emotional problem, wait until the primary problem has been assessed first or probe for it only when the client is not making the expected progress on his primary problem.

Key Point

Be alert for the possible presence of meta-emotional problems.

51 Assuming that the meta-emotional problem is always present

Determining whether or not a meta-emotional problem is present is part of the REBT assessment process. However, determining (e.g. 'I wonder if there is one?') does not mean predetermining (i.e. 'It'll be there'). The REBT literature does say that clients frequently disturb themselves about their emotional problems, but some trainees convert 'frequently' into 'always'. This can lead you to pressurizing the client to 'confess' to her 'other problem':

Trainee: Now, do you experience other feelings in relation to your anxiety?

Client: What do you mean?

Trainee: Do you, for example, get angry for having this anxiety problem?

Client: Sometimes.

Trainee: So you feel angry about feeling anxious, and this anger will interfere with our focus on your anxiety. Right?

Client: No, I wouldn't say that at all.

Trainee: Okay. Do you see your anxiety as a sign of personal weakness? Do you try and hide it from others?

Client: I certainly don't shout about it from the rooftops, if that's what you mean.

Trainee: So, do you feel ashamed about having this problem?

Client: If I was that ashamed, I wouldn't be here, would I?

Trainee: Shame is often a problem with people who are experiencing emotional problems.

Client: But I'm not really ashamed about being anxious.

Trainee: When you say 'not really', does that mean you are to some extent?

Client: (exasperated) No!

Trainee: Okay, so you are definitely not feeling ashamed. Do you feel depressed about this continuing anxiety in your life?

[The trainee is dogmatically determined to work his way through REBT's lexicon of unhealthy negative emotions to pinpoint a meta-emotional problem. The trainee has lost sight of the fact that hypothesis testing is carried out in an open-minded way, not a close-minded one.]

Key Point

Remember that meta-emotional problems may be present but not always so. Be open-minded in looking for their presence.

52 Always working on a meta-emotional problem first

If you have detected a meta-emotional problem, then it does not automatically follow that you should start working on it there and then. I (WD) have advanced four criteria for working on the client's meta-emotional problem before his primary emotional problem:

1. When the meta-emotional problem interferes with your work on the primary problem.
2. When the presence of the meta-emotional problem interferes with the client's between-sessions task assignments on his primary problem.
3. When the meta-emotional problem is clinically more important than the primary problem.
4. When the client sees the sense of tackling his meta-emotional problem before his primary problem.

Unfortunately, the trainee does not pay any attention to these criteria when she arbitrarily decides to work first on the client's anger about his performance anxiety:

Trainee: Now, what do you get angry about with regard to your performance anxiety?

Client: I get angry with myself for having this problem in the first place. I should be able to run a workshop without any anxiety, but I realize I've got the problem, so I'd better deal with it.

[The client is indicating that he would not be distracted from working on his anxiety by his anger.]

Trainee: So you have the anger-producing belief 'I should be able to run a workshop without anxiety'. If we can get you to accept, without anger, the grim reality of your anxiety, then we can focus on your anxiety.

Client: We can focus on it now. I am angry about it but not at the moment.

Trainee: You could become angry again, and then we'd have to deal with it, which would pull us off the anxiety. Better to deal with it now, get it out of the way so we won't be distracted by it.

Client: I'm not angry, but, if I become angry, then I'll let you know whether it's interfering with things.

Trainee: As I said, better to deal with it now and get it out of the way.

[The client does not see the sense in working on his meta-emotional problem first, but the trainee seems determined that the client should see things her way. The therapeutic relationship is likely to be damaged if this friction continues.]

Key Point

Only work on the meta-emotional problem first if one or more of the four criteria are met.

PART III:
GOAL-SETTING ERRORS

53 Not seeing the relevance of two goal-setting stages

There are usually two goal-setting stages in the initial assessment of your client's presenting problem:

1. When the client states his problem and goal in general terms (the 'problem as defined').
2. Ater the problem has been explored in ABC terms and the problem and goal have now been made specific (the 'problem as assessed').

Trainees often overlook the second stage of goal setting and wonder why it is important, if they already have a goal:

Supervisor: What is the client's general goal?

Trainee: To overcome his procrastination.

Supervisor: And, when you had assessed his procrastination, what did you find?

Trainee: That he's anxious about handing in a poor essay and seeing himself as a failure, if it is judged as poor. That's why he procrastinates.

Supervisor: Those are the factors maintaining his procrastination. Now you need to set new goals with him that target those maintaining factors. Why do you think you need to do that?

Trainee: To help him, and me, see that the specific goals are to help him move from anxiety to concern, or whatever term he wants to use, and accept the possibility of handing in a poor essay without condemning himself as a failure.

Supervisor: So, if the client can achieve these specific goals . . . ?

Trainee: Then these will help him to achieve his general goal of overcoming his procrastination. Now I see the relevance of two goal-setting stages.

Supervisor: Good, and help your clients to see the relevance, if they are unsure about it.

Key Point

Goal setting occurs when the client's problem is defined *and* after it has been assessed.

---

54 Only focusing on clients' long-term goals, instead of achieving a balance between short- and long-term goals

REBT argues that we are likely to be at our happiest when enjoying the pleasures of the moment and planning constructively for the future (known as long-range hedonism). Clients often pursue short-term goals (e.g. avoidance), which sabotage their long-term goals (e.g. overcoming their anxiety). On the other hand, some trainees only focus on long-term goals thereby implying that short-term goals are unimportant or self-defeating:

Trainee: You're falling behind with your studies because you go to too many parties. Is that right?

Client: Yes.

Trainee: So pleasure always first, then work a distant second, and sometimes you never get down to it at all.

Client: A good party versus studying alone on some boring subject. No contest.

Trainee: Do you want to pass your exams? (client nods) Then I would suggest you stop all party-going and concentrate on hard study. When the exams are out of the way, then go to parties. Does that sound like a worthwhile goal to work for?

Client: Are you joking about the goal? Stop all party-going?

[The client is not interested in the goal as it is extreme (i.e. all work and no play) and hardly likely to motivate him to change.]

In this extract, the therapist looks at a goal that involves both work and play:

Therapist: What about study during the week and parties only at the weekend, but you don't go the parties when you don't study?

Client: Yes, I can live with that.

Therapist: So let's look at developing an attitude that will help you to study more and party less.

Key Point

Help your clients to reach a balance between pursuing both short- and long-term goals.

---

55 Setting a goal that would help to perpetuate the client's irrational beliefs

Self-helping goals in REBT are those that involve healthy negative emotions and productive behaviours underpinned by rational beliefs. You might unwittingly set a goal with your client that actually perpetuates her irrational beliefs:

Client: He dumped me. I'm nothing without him and I can't live without him. I'll do anything to get him to take me back. I'll beg, if I have to.

Trainee: So, is that the goal you would like us to work on: to get him to take you back?

['To get him to take you back' is within her partner's control, not hers – see Point 56.]

Client: That's what I want most of all.

Trainee: Let's see what you need to change about yourself so he'll take you back.

In this dialogue, the therapist explains why he thinks the client's goal is self-defeating and disturbance prolonging and suggests an alternative one:

Therapist: If I go along with your goal, then all I'm doing is agreeing with you that you can't live without him, you're nothing without him, and it's all right to grovel before him, begging to be taken back. I wouldn't be helping you to overcome your emotional problems, I'd be helping you to make them worse. What if he doesn't take you back?

Client: I don't want to think about that.

Therapist: Okay, think about this then: just imagine that you could live without him and be reasonably happy, and stopped believing you are nothing without him, how would you then feel?

Client: Well, I suppose I'd be much less upset.

Therapist: And, if you still wanted to get back with him, would you beg?

Client: No. I would ask, but I wouldn't beg.

Therapist: What would be the difference?

Client: If I asked, that would mean I have self-respect and could live without him, but begging means no self-respect and continuing to be his slave or throwing myself in the river, if he says 'no'.

Therapist: So would you like to work towards a goal where you asked but not begged?

['Asked' is conceptualized by the therapist as being based on healthy negative emotions and rational beliefs, which he will presently explain to the client. In our experience, when some clients get to the point of asking, they are no longer interested in the old relationship and choose a partner that reflects their new-and-improved self-image.]

Client: I would like to try that.

[The client is now receptive to seeing other ways of dealing with her emotional disturbance.]

Key Point

Do not select goals that perpetuate your client's irrational beliefs.

56 Agreeing on goals that are outside of the client's control

Clients' goals for change are often placed in others' hands (e.g. 'If she treats me better, then I can feel better') thereby reinforcing their own sense of powerlessness or victim status (others are often unaware of this 'power' that has been given to them). It is important to teach your clients what is within their power to change or control and what is not; this teaching is missing in this dialogue:

Client: Now that I'm self-employed, I've got to get some work. I haven't got too much money left to pay the bills. I wish some of these companies would give me some bloody work. I'm pissed off with the time it's taking.

Trainee: So, your goal is to get some work from some of these companies?

Client: That's right. They give me some work and I'll feel a whole lot better.

Trainee: So, let me make a note of this goal we're working towards.

Client: Some of these companies make it really hard to promote yourself, you know, things like not returning your phone calls or letters.

[The client spends a lot of the session complaining about these companies as if this will somehow bring her closer to her goal.]

You might think that 'getting some work' is a perfectly reasonable goal, but the therapist discusses the problem with it:

Therapist: Who actually gives you the work: you or someone in the company you're targeting for the work?

Client: Well, someone in the company.

Therapist: Is that within your control or theirs?

Client: Theirs.

Therapist: What is within your control?

Client: Keeping pushing myself forward, not giving up, learning from people who have been self-employed longer than me, that sort of thing.

Therapist: And do you do those things?

Client: No. I suppose I'm expecting quick results and not prepared for the long haul or taking setbacks very well.

[This reply could indicate the client is adhering to a philosophy of low frustration tolerance.]

Therapist: So, if you learnt to be persistent and resilient in facing these difficulties, what then?

[The antidote to LFT is learning a philosophy of high frustration tolerance (HFT).]

Client: I suppose I'll be more likely to get work, but no guarantees.

Therapist: So shall we start developing an outlook based on persistence and resilience, something that is within your control?

Client: Okay. I do want to succeed in my new career.

Therapist: Having the right attitude in trying to get the work is just as important as having the talent to do the work when you get it.

With regard to client goals targeted at changing others, it is important to point out that clients usually have to change first (e.g. become more assertive) before attempting to influence the behaviour of others. Change is within the other person's control, and attempting to influence the other person to change is within the client's control.

Key Point

Ensure that clients' goals are within their sphere of control.

57 Not stating the client's goals in positive terms

Clients often state their goals as the absence or reduction of a negative state: for example, 'I don't want to feel guilty any more' or 'I want to feel less anxious'. These goals state how the client does not want to feel or behave (i.e. stated in negative terms), instead of how the client wants to feel or behave (i.e. stated in positive terms). Stating goals in positive terms

> is very important because of the role that goal setting plays in human cognition and performance . . . When the goal is stated positively, clients are more likely to encode and rehearse the things they want to be able to do rather than the things they want to avoid or stop (Cormier and Cormier, 1985: 223).

In this dialogue, the trainee does not pick up that the goal is stated in negative terms:

Client: I want to stop feeling anxious and not blush when I'm the centre of attention. Just stop acting like an idiot because people are looking at me.

Trainee: So that's the goal you'll be moving towards.

Actually, that is what the client will be moving away from. What she is moving towards is clarified by the therapist:

Therapist: If you want to stop feeling anxious and acting like an 'idiot', how do you want to feel and behave?

Client: I'd like to feel concerned about being the centre of attention and stay in the situation instead of trying to avoid it.

Therapist: And what belief will accompany this feeling of concern?

Client: That I can accept being the centre of attention without liking it and accept myself for blushing or acting awkwardly. Do you know what I'd really like to feel in that situation?

Therapist: What's that?

Client: I really want to feel relaxed and confident. Let people look because I'm no longer bothered. That sounds good. I'd really like to achieve those things.

Therapist: Okay. That may be possible, and it would probably take two goal-setting stages to achieve. First is to overcome your psychological problem by feeling concerned, not anxious, about being the centre of attention. When you have achieved that, then you can set a personal development goal whereby you feel relaxed and confident when people look at you: you no longer feel concerned when you are the centre of attention.

Client: Good. Let's get working on stage one then.

Key Point

Ensure that your clients' goals are stated in positive terms, not in negative terms, and are based on rational ideas. Sometimes clients will have two goals in mind: overcoming their psychological problem and then focusing on some aspect of personal development.

58 Focusing on process goals instead of outcome goals

Some clients come to therapy to immerse themselves in self-exploration (therapeutic process) rather than setting specific goals for change (therapeutic outcome). REBT is problem focused and outcome orientated; if you focus on process, therapy is likely to get bogged down in endless self-analysis and 'feeling talk' (see Point 27):

Supervisor: Listening to the session tape, I don't get the impression your client has been introduced to REBT yet.

Trainee: That's true. He wanted so much to find out why his life is in such a mess, and we've got stuck on it. I don't know how to intervene to set the goals.

Supervisor: To move him from interminable problem describing to problem solving. How do you begin to do that?

Trainee: Tactfully interrupt him to start with. I suppose I could say to him what goals would he need to pull himself out of the mess, instead of just talking about the mess.

Supervisor: Good. Also, point out to him that working towards those goals not only helps to pull him out of the mess but also helps him to understand how he got into it.

Trainee: Sounds simple when you say it.

Supervisor: Try it and see what happens. I'll look forward to hearing the results on your next tape.

Key Point

Focus on outcome goals, not process goals.

59 Focusing on practical goals and neglecting emotional goals

REBT advocates that clients face A in an undisturbed manner at C before turning to practical problem solving. For example, a person who is angry with a colleague who behaves obnoxiously towards him is encouraged to undisturb himself about the behaviour before deciding on his next step, which might be to learn assertiveness or leave the job – the decision would be made in an undisturbed state. Focusing only on a practical goal, like leaving the job, leaves the emotional disturbance intact (e.g. 'I absolutely shouldn't have to be subject to this behaviour. It's awful') and ready to 'strike' again, if the client meets others who behave in a similar manner towards him. The trainee in this dialogue agrees with the practical goal advanced by the client:

Client: The relationship is boring. I've been in quite a few of them. 'Get the hell out', that's what I say.

Trainee: Seems the sensible thing to do. Do you ever think you could try to make it more interesting, put more effort into it?

Client: If it's boring, it's boring. Why waste time and effort? Pack your bags and leave.

Trainee: I suppose you're right. I can't see any reasons to stay, if it really is that boring.

The therapist can see some 'reasons to stay' in this extract:

Therapist: Does it ever bother that you leave a relationship as soon as it gets boring?

Client: Why should I stay?

Therapist: What's the attitude you have to boredom in relationships?

Client: I can't stand it. I like excitement: things happening all the time. I know it sounds childish and I know I'm running away from responsibility, but there it is.

Therapist: Would you like to learn to stay in a so-called boring relationship, put up with these unpleasant feelings until they pass and then decide whether you want to stay or leave? You might even find things in the relationship to enjoy that you wouldn't be aware of because you're usually long gone.

Client: I wouldn't have to stay after I got over the boredom, would I?

Therapist: You don't have to stay but the point is your choice will be made on the basis of emotional stability, not emotional disturbance. You can prove to yourself that you can tolerate boredom and thereby stop turning a relationship hassle into an 'I've-got-to-get-out-of-here' horror.

Do not overlook practical goals after the emotional ones have been achieved: your clients still want to achieve other things in life apart from overcoming their emotional difficulties.

Key Point

Remember to focus on emotional goals before practical goals.

---

60 Helping clients to seek only intellectual insight into their problems

REBT distinguishes between intellectual and emotional insight. The former refers to rational beliefs lightly and intermittently held and the latter to rational beliefs deeply and consistently held. Practising a rational outlook helps clients to move from intellectual to emotional insight. Some clients believe that, if they knew why they feel and behave as they do, this would bring a spontaneous improvement in their present functioning without any further effort on their part. In this dialogue, the trainee appears to believe this too:

Supervisor: Listening to the tape, you are spending a lot of time discussing the client's past history. To what end?

Trainee: The client wants to know why he suffers from panic attacks, why did it happen to him.

Supervisor: And, if he is able to gain this understanding, will that help him to enter those situations he currently avoids in case he has a panic attack?

Trainee: I think he will feel better with this understanding. It will reassure him and put his problems into an historical context: dispel the mystery.

Supervisor: But will he get better because of it? Will this understanding get him out of the house and into those avoided situations?

Trainee: I suppose, thinking about it now, no, it won't. Just a better understanding of his panic is not going to help him overcome his panic.

Supervisor: So the next step is to move from insight to action.

Trainee: You mean encourage him to go into those situations and stay in them until his panic attacks subside? So that he can conquer his panic with new attitudes and behaviours? The emotional insight stage?

Supervisor: Exactly. And encourage him to enter those situations every day, not just occasionally.

Trainee: I can see the sense of that.

Teach your clients that intellectual insight plus forceful and persistent daily action brings about therapeutic change. Gaining intellectual insight is the precursor to emotional insight, not the goal of therapy.

Key Point

Show your clients why intellectual insight alone is insufficient to bring about personal change; both forms of insight are required.

---

61 Helping clients to feel neutral about negative events

When clients say they want to feel indifferent or not care about adverse events in their lives, this attitude may appear helpful at first glance. Some trainees go along with this client goal in the mistaken belief that, if you do not care about something, then the problem will disappear. In our experience, clients usually do care, and you might be helping them to suppress their healthy desires for bad things not to occur in their lives as the therapist points out:

Therapist: You're trying to convince me that you don't give a damn about losing your job. Is that really true?

Client: If I do give a damn, then I'll be all torn up inside about it. So, it's better to feel nothing.

Therapist: Isn't the reverse true: you do actually feel something? If I can help you to accept the grim reality of losing your job but without being 'all torn up inside about it', just disappointed for example, would you be prepared to feel something instead of nothing?

Client: I suppose so. I know that I'm lying to myself about feeling nothing.

Therapist: And I don't want to help you reinforce that pretence because it's self-defeating in the long run.

Key Point

Help your clients to experience healthy negative emotions about adverse life events.

---

62 Implying a cure can be attained rather than focusing on improved problem management

A cure may be the ideal of therapeutic intervention, but improvement is the usual reality. Improvement can be measured along the following three dimensions:

1. Frequency – does the problem occur less frequently than before?
2. Intensity – is the problem less severe/intense than before?
3. Duration – does the problem last for shorter periods than before?

While you probably would not explicitly agree to providing a 'cure', you may implicitly do so:

Client: I've had such problems with my sleep over the years. It's been so draining, so exhausting. I can't tell you what I've been through. I would love to have an uninterrupted eight hours' sleep every night for the rest of my life. Wouldn't that be wonderful?

Trainee: That would indeed be wonderful. Let's see what we can do.

If the client believes that such a goal is both possible to achieve and you have agreed to it, he could hold you to account for your pledge when his 'wonderful' goal remains elusive (e.g. 'You promised me I would have uninterrupted sleep every night. I've been in therapy for three months now, and I'm still not there. When will I be?').

Key Point

Set goals that are explicit, not implicit, and are realistic and achievable, using the three dimensions of frequency, intensity and duration.

---

63 Agreeing with clients' goals that are unrealistically ambitious or unrealistically unambitious

Clients' goals should help them to tackle their problems constructively, instead of reinforcing them. For example, a client with perfectionist tendencies may set her goal too high (e.g. 'I must not make any mistakes on these forthcoming projects; if I do, this will mean I'm an abysmal failure') thereby making it unachievable, prolonging her procrastination about starting these projects and strengthening her fear of failure. You may believe that there are ways of avoiding all mistakes and convey to the client that she can be infallible, if she finds the 'right' strategy (watch your own perfectionist leanings). With such clients, it is important to help them set goals that acknowledge their fallibility, deal effectively with setbacks and strive for ambitious standards but not unrealistic ones. Clients who are unambitious in their goal setting also usually fear failure, which the trainee does not discuss in this dialogue:

Client: I just want to scrape through my exams. The bottom grade will be fine.

Trainee: Obviously you've got to do some work, if you want to obtain even a bottom grade. Do you think you will scrape through with a bottom grade?

[The trainee could have asked why the client is setting her sights so low.]

Client: Yes. No sweat.

Such clients are hardly likely to be elated by attaining their goals:

> the result is usually as inconsequential as the goal itself and often feels like a 'hollow victory' with no sense of accomplishment . . . Challenging goals are more likely to lead to higher performance than 'easy goals' (Cormier and Cormier, 1985: 224).

Key Point

Help your clients to set goals that are neither overwhelmingly high nor underwhelmingly low. Tackle the irrational ideas that impel your clients to set such goals.

64 Not eliciting from your client a commitment to change

Stating a goal is not the same as being committed to achieving it, e.g. a client states his goal as abstinence from alcohol, but this goal was 'forced' on him by his wife threatening to leave; he wants her to stay and for himself to continue drinking. To be committed to change means undertaking willingly the hard work involved in reaching the goal and seeing clearly the benefits to be gained when the goal is achieved. In this dialogue, the trainee assumes that stating a goal is a commitment to realizing it:

Trainee: What goal are we working towards then?

Client: I suppose I'd better do something about this temper of mine.

[Hardly a ringing declaration of commitment . . .]

Trainee: What specifically are you going to do about it?

[. . . which the trainee does not point out. She could have asked: 'What do you mean by "I suppose"?']

Client: Well, get it under more control so I'm not lashing out when I get frustrated. I'm sure my temper is not as bad as people make out.

[The client's last comment is another ambivalent statement about change.]

Trainee: Okay. Let's start looking at anger-management strategies.

In order for your client to be committed to a goal, I (WD) believe it is important for you to help him first evaluate fully the advantages and disadvantages of both the problem state and the alternative-goal state. Through a cost–benefit analysis of the pros and cons of changing, the client may decide that the goal is more attractive than plodding on with the problem.

At this point, you can ask your client for a commitment to the goal. The client is now more likely to be motivated to change rather than still ambivalent about it:

Client: I never realized how much grief my anger outbursts caused others or myself until you did that cost–benefit thing; it really brought it home to me. I don't have to be a wimp if I stop being angry; in fact, I'll probably end up a stronger person if I learn to control my temper. I'll certainly give it a go.

Key Point

Ensure that you elicit from your client a commitment to change, not just a statement of his goals. If your client is ambivalent about achieving his goals, carry out a cost–benefit analysis to increase his motivation to change.

PART IV:
DISPUTING ERRORS

65 Not preparing your clients for disputing

Disputing clients' irrational beliefs is probably the principal activity of experienced REBT therapists (Neenan and Dryden, 2000). Disputing can be an uncomfortable or unnerving experience for clients as they are, in essence, being asked to defend their beliefs. In order to pave the way for disputing and avoid the impression that you are attacking your clients, there are a number of activities to carry out.

First, review the ABC of the specific example of your client's target problem; this refreshes his mind about it. Second, ensure that your client understands the B–C connection; this will help him to see the sense in disputing B. Third, help him to see that his new C (goal) is achieved by changing B: emotional change flows from cognitive change. Fourth, explain to your client what is involved in the disputing process (i.e. an examination of his irrational belief) and what is not involved (e.g. arguing, 'brainwashing').

Unfortunately, some trainees are so eager to get 'stuck in' to disputing that they forget the importance of this preparatory stage and give the appearance of 'pouncing' on their clients. This usually has the effect of putting clients on the defensive or being bewildered by the trainee's behaviour:

Trainee: Why must you not make mistakes?

Client: What do you mean? I don't understand.

Trainee: I'm disputing your irrational belief.

Client: My what?

Trainee: Your irrational belief. We identified it in the previous session.

Client: I can't remember.

[This reply emphasizes the importance of reviewing the ABC example before disputing commences.]

Trainee: You know, why you mustn't make mistakes. That's what we're disputing.

Client: Is it? Why are we doing that?

[At this point, the trainee should suspend disputing and retrace his steps with the client to determine where they parted company.]

Key Point

Prepare your clients for the disputing process. Do not just plunge into it.

---

66 Disputing in a mechanical manner

Irrational beliefs are disputed in four major ways, focusing on:

1. Flexibility vs. rigidity (e.g. the premise belief 'I must succeed' is rigid because it does not incorporate possible failure), and extreme or non-extreme (e.g. the derivative belief 'I'm useless' is extreme because it does not acknowledge our fallibility and complexity as human beings).
2. Logic. Does it logically follow that, because you want to succeed, therefore you must succeed? This is an example of a non sequitur, i.e. an argument in which the conclusion does not follow logically from the premises that precede it.
3. Empiricism. Does your client's demand for success correspond with empirical reality? If the world obeyed her demand, then she would be guaranteed success. Does the evidence support this view or contradict it?
4. Pragmatism. Does your client's irrational belief help her to attain her goals? What are the consequences for her of holding on to the belief 'I must succeed'?

In our experience, trainees frequently dispute their clients' irrational beliefs in a mechanical manner, as if they were reading the questions from an REBT textbook and paying little, if any, attention to the clients' actual replies:

Trainee: Is your belief 'I must not make mistakes' rigid or flexible?

Client: Sounds as if it is rigid.

Trainee: Rigid then. Now, does it logically follow that, because you don't want to make mistakes, you must not make them?

Client: I suppose it might sound a little nonsensical.

Trainee: Right, illogical then. Now where's the evidence for this belief?

Client: I'm not sure.

Trainee: There isn't any, is there? Now where is it going to get you holding on to this belief?

Client: Well, it's not all bad.

Trainee: So nowhere then.

[The trainee then goes on to dispute the client's derivative belief, 'I'm a failure', in the same mechanical way.]

The trainee might now think: 'That's the disputing done. Now on to the homework.' To avoid mechanical disputing, familiarize yourself with the points you need to raise and the questions you need to ask and elaborate on (see, for example, Dryden, 1996; Neenan and Dryden, 2000; Walen et al., 1992). Use the four types of arguments in disputing your own irrational beliefs and practise disputing with other trainees or friends. Through these methods, you should be able to ask disputing questions as if they are a natural part of your enquiring mind and not programmed into you. Finally, when you see disputing as a challenge and no longer a chore, you may actually pay attention to your clients' replies.

Key Point

Develop a genuine enthusiasm for disputing.

---

67 Only disputing either the premise or the derivative belief

An irrational belief in REBT terms consists of a rigid premise (absolute musts or shoulds) and one or more extreme derivative (awfulizing, low frustration tolerance, and depreciation of self and/or others). Only disputing either the premise or the derivative part of the irrational belief means that the undisputed part remains intact. Some trainees assume that by disputing musts the derivative belief will naturally wither away, or through tackling self-depreciation, for example, clients will automatically stop making demands upon themselves or others. Though the undisputed part of the belief may be weakened by the indirect effects from the disputed part of the belief, this cannot be taken for granted and a weakened irrational belief is still an irrational belief:

Client: I can see and feel the benefits of giving up these ludicrous demands I make on myself, but I can't shake off this idea that I am still a failure to some extent, if things don't go right for me.

Trainee: That's because there are probably a few demands still lurking about up here (tapping forehead) that you haven't dealt with yet. Once they're sent packing, the idea that you're a failure will fade away.

[What is required is an examination of the client's self-depreciation belief, not reassurance.]

Client: Hmm. I hope so.

After you have disputed both parts of an irrational belief, your client might tell you that he finds it easier to understand why his derivative belief is irrational than why his must is irrational or vice versa. If this is the case, then direct your disputing questions to this part of the belief as this strategy is more likely to promote therapeutic progress than spending equal time on both parts of the belief.

Key Point

Dispute both parts of your clients' irrational beliefs. However, some clients will find that disputing the premise is more meaningful for them than disputing the derivative and vice versa.

68 Using didactic disputing when Socratic disputing would be more productive and vice versa

There are two major disputing styles in REBT: Socratic and didactic. Socratic disputing involves you asking your clients questions regarding the logical, empirical and pragmatic status of their irrational beliefs and whether these beliefs are rigid or flexible (see Point 66). Socratic disputing is designed to help clients reflect on their beliefs; through this process, clients come to the eventual realization that their irrational beliefs are self-defeating. Didactic disputing (technically speaking, it is teaching you are undertaking) involves you presenting brief explanations to your clients as to why their irrational beliefs are irrational. REBT therapists usually employ both disputing styles. It is important that you assess which disputing style is more productive with each client rather than move between the two styles when the mood takes you. In this dialogue, the trainee is being heavily didactic and long-winded without assessing the impact of this on the client or whether the client would be better engaged in Socratic dialogue:

Trainee: One way of testing our beliefs to determine whether they are rational or irrational is by looking for evidence: does our thinking correspond to empirical reality or, to put it another way, is our thinking consistent with reality? So, with your demand that others must treat you fairly, we treat this belief as an hypothesis rather than as a fact, and we search for the evidence to confirm or disconfirm your belief, and then we evaluate the evidence to see –

Client: (impatiently) In essence, we are going to determine whether my belief is realistic or unrealistic. Right?

[The client has condensed the trainee's long-windedness to a sentence and demonstrated he can think these issues through for himself. The trainee should now switch to Socratic disputing by asking, for example: 'Is your belief realistic or unrealistic and why?']

151

Trainee: That's exactly right. Now, as I was saying, we evaluate the evidence to see whether it does support your belief that other people must treat you fairly . . .

[The client has to suffer more of this before informing the trainee that he has a brain, and he can use it, if the trainee will give him a chance.]

On the other hand, you can be too Socratic by asking lots of questions that the client cannot answer; instead of putting her out of her 'misery' with some answers for her to consider, you provide 'a slow death by a thousand questions' approach:

Trainee: Why must you succeed?

Client: Because it's very nice to succeed.

[The client has said why it is desirable to succeed but has not answered the question why she *must* succeed.]

Trainee: You answered a question I didn't ask you. So, why must you succeed?

[The trainee should have explained what he meant by his statement – the client is providing evidence for her rational desires, not for her irrational musts.]

Client: Because good things come from success, you feel good. Isn't that enough?

Trainee: Why must you succeed?

Client: Who doesn't want to succeed in life?

Trainee: Yes, I understand that, but that doesn't answer the question: why must you succeed?

[The trainee thinks if he keeps repeating this question, the client will 'see the light'.]

Client: (becoming angry) I've told you why I must succeed.

[The client is not grasping the point Socratically; so a brief didactic explanation would be much more welcome at this juncture such as: 'The point of my question is this: if the world obeyed your demands, then you would succeed at whatever and whenever you demanded. Nothing could prevent you from succeeding. Now, does the world obey your demands?' If the client does not grasp this point, another brief explanation is required.]

In deciding upon a predominatly Socratic or didactic style of disputing, assess your client's intellectual abilities (e.g. unreflective clients might do better with a more didactic style while psychologically minded clients might profit more with a mainly Socratic style). Generally speaking, you can start with Socratic disputing supplemented by short didactic explanations until incoming information tells you to retain or alter this strategy.

Key Point

Assess your clients' responses to Socratic and didactic disputing to determine which style is the more productive for them.

---

69 Not focusing on the type of argument that is more helpful to your client than the other types

Initially, you can dispute your client's irrational belief using logical, empirical and pragmatic arguments. Clients do not usually find all three types of arguments equally helpful or insightful. When it becomes apparent to you which type(s) of argument your client responds to, then phase out the one(s) that is less productive. In this dialogue, the trainee persists with logical arguments, even though the client is impervious to this form of questioning:

Trainee: How does it follow logically that, because you failed to get the job, you are failure?

Client: I don't know. What do you mean by 'follow logically'?

Trainee: Well, it's the way you reason things out. You failed to get the job, which is true, and then you jump to this sweeping conclusion that this makes you a failure. So, does it follow? Does it make sense to say that?

Client: In my mind it does.

Trainee: Would you condemn your best friend in the same way, if he failed to get a job?

Client: No, but then he's not me, is he?

Trainee: Is it inconsistent in your thinking to condemn yourself but not him for the same thing?

Client: Look, I don't really know what you're going on about, to be honest.

In the following dialogue, the therapist reviews the three types of arguments with the client:

Therapist: What did you think of the logical approach?

Client: Not much. It went over my head.

Therapist: And the realistic arguments about if you were really a failure, then all you could ever do would be to fail?

Client: I could see what you were driving at but still too much up in the air, you know what I mean?

Therapist: I do. The pragmatic arguments were about how your life is likely to be, if you hold on to that belief. I thought those arguments were helpful for you. Am I correct?

Client: You are. When you were asking me those sorts of questions, something clicked. I could imagine myself moping around like a miserable git for the rest of my life. I don't want that.

Therapist: Shall we stick with those kinds of questions?

Client: Yes, because that really brings it home to me.

In our experience, pragmatic arguments are the most persuasive because they itemize for clients the concrete consequences of continuing to adhere to irrational beliefs.

Key Point

Discover which type of disputing strategy your clients find the most influential in challenging and changing their irrational beliefs.

70 Not helping your client to state a full rational belief to negate their irrational belief

When a client says 'I would greatly prefer to get the job', it may seem like she has stated a rational belief but this would be misleading. She has only stated a partial rational belief. How will this belief be completed: by negating the demand or reinforcing it? By asking the client to complete the sentence you will find out: 'I would greatly prefer to get the job, and therefore I have to.' A promising rational belief returned to its irrational state. Negating the demand requires a full rational belief: 'I would greatly prefer to get the job, but there is no reason why I must get it.' Partial rational statements can also be present in derivative beliefs, e.g. 'I did not get the job – but this does not prove I'm incompetent.' What does it prove then? Again, you need to ask the client to complete the sentence, e.g. 'I did not get the job, but this does not mean I'm incompetent. It means I'm barely adequate.' Implicit self-depreciation, not self-acceptance, has been made explicit (for a detailed discussion of partial and full rational beliefs, see Neenan and Dryden, 1999). Encouraging clients to state only partial rational beliefs is common among trainees:

Trainee: How would you state your rational response to rejection?

Client: I would strongly prefer not to be rejected.

Trainee: Good. And the self-acceptance belief?

[It is not 'good', as she might be endorsing an irrational belief.]

Client: If I am rejected, this does not mean I'm worthless.

[What does it mean then?]

Trainee: Now you've just stated what we call in REBT a 'rational belief'.

[Only by ascertaining a full preference belief and a full self-acceptance belief can the trainee be confident that he has obtained a rational belief

156

from his client. This belief is: 'I would strongly prefer not to be rejected, but I'm not immune from rejection. If I am rejected, it does not mean I'm worthless. What it does mean is that I can learn to accept myself, irrespective of how others see or treat me.']

Once these full rational beliefs have been stated, then the client can collapse them into more manageable and idiosyncratic terms (see Point 71).

Key Point

Ensure that you encourage your clients to state full rational beliefs, not partial ones.

---

71 Not helping your client to construct a rational alternative to the irrational belief

As your client struggles to give up her irrational belief, what will replace it? If nothing is on offer, why bother expending the effort to change? As DiGiuseppe observes:

> Challenging irrational beliefs is not sufficient to change them. People frequently hold on to beliefs that they know are logically flawed and do not lead to accurate predictions of reality, but no alternative ideas are available to replace the flawed idea. The history of science is filled with such examples. People do not give up ideas, regardless of the evidence against the idea, unless they have an alternative idea to replace it (1991: 181).

Some trainees omit this crucial discussion of constructing an alternative belief with their clients:

Trainee: Disputing chips away at your irrational belief until it's weakened to the point of virtual extinction.

Client: Then what?

Trainee: Well, you'll be less emotionally disturbed for a start and no longer plagued by demands.

Client: It's a strange thing to say, but some of my beliefs, like the demand for approval, felt strangely reassuring in some ways. They were part of me. It's weird giving them up. It's like leaving what you've been familiar with, but you don't know what lies ahead.

Trainee: Don't worry, you'll get used to it.

What is it that the client will get used to? The absence of rational beliefs to guide her through present and future difficulties? The therapist rectifies this omission in the following excerpt:

Therapist: If you give up the irrational belief, presumably you want to put a rational or more helpful belief in its place?

Client: That would be a good start.

Therapist: So, if you gave up these perfectionist demands, how would you now like to see yourself while still striving for your high standards?

Client: What really interests me is the pursuit of excellence.

Therapist: How does that differ from perfectionism?

[The therapist wants to check that the client is not replacing an old irrational idea with a new one.]

Client: Well, it means that I won't be afraid to fail, learn from my mistakes, stop avoiding projects I might fail at, and the energy I spent on avoiding will now be spent on more doing.

Therapist: And what about if you do fail at times?

Client: I like the idea of being self-accepting. Don't throw yourself into the dustbin because of setbacks. All this sounds good, but how do I get it?

Therapist: You've already started the process by articulating your new ideas.

When your clients do articulate their new rational ideas, make sure it is in their language rather than in the lengthy and somewhat unwieldy statements found in some REBT textbooks, e.g. 'I would prefer to have your approval, but there is no reason why I must have your approval, and, if I don't receive your approval, this does not mean I am inadequate but a fallible human being who can accept himself despite not being accepted by others.' The client's rational belief might be 'Too bad', which, when analysed, is based on a fully stated preferential belief (see point 70) and self-acceptance. The philosophy behind the words is more important than the words themselves; so do not 'force' your clients into uttering unnatural pronouncements.

However, do ensure that your clients' stated rational beliefs do reflect the meaning behind the 'lengthy and somewhat unwieldy' formally stated rational beliefs.

Key Point

It is crucial that you help your clients to develop rational alternatives to their irrational beliefs, if therapeutic change is to occur.

72 Not disputing the rational belief in the same way as the irrational belief

Merely stating a rational belief is not the same process as understanding why it is rational or believing in it. To promote understanding of what actually constitutes rationality in REBT terms, your clients will need to dispute their rational beliefs in the same way as their irrational ones. Some trainees believe that, if clients articulate rational statements, they will automatically internalize a rational outlook:

Trainee: If you write down your rational statement on a card, keep the card with you so you can read the statement if you run into any emotional problems, and that will help you to think more clearly in dealing with them. Okay?

Client: Er, is that it? Just keep saying it to myself and I'll start thinking differently?

Trainee: Well, it doesn't happen overnight. It takes time to sink in. You'll start seeing positive changes in your thinking.

[Or maybe nothing will happen as the client parrots rational statements without understanding the principles on which they are based.]

You need to apply the four criteria of rationality to the client's premise belief to determine whether it is rational, as the therapist does here:

Therapist: Your belief is 'I would prefer not to blush in front of others, but there is no reason why I must not blush in front of others'. Is that belief rigid or flexible?

[When the therapist turns her attention to the client's derivative belief to determine whether it is rational, she will ask him whether his belief is extreme or non-extreme.]

Client: It's flexible, because it supports my preference while not discounting the possibility that I might do so.

160

Therapist: Is your belief logical, or, more simply, does it make sense?

Client: It does make sense, but I can't spell it out in terms of logic. Trust me on that.

Therapist: Well, just to spell it out: because you flexibly don't want to blush in front of others, you are not jumping to the illogical conclusion that therefore you rigidly must not do so. Your reasoning is logical. Logical arguments can often be difficult to grasp.

Client: Let me think about it.

Therapist: Is your belief realistic?

Client: Yes, because I can't control reality to obey my demands. If I blush, I blush.

Therapist: Is your belief helpful?

Client: I think it will be helpful, because I'll be more relaxed around others instead of worrying about whether I'll blush or not. I'll need a few more weeks yet before I can give you a proper answer to that question.

The therapist then applies the four criteria of rationality to the client's derivative belief: 'If I blush in front of others, this proves I'm a fallible human being, not an inadequate one.' You can audiotape your disputing sessions so clients can consider the arguments in greater depth between sessions.

Key Point

Dispute your clients' rational belief in the same way you would dispute their irrational belief.

73 Not having order in disputing

When you are disputing your client's irrational belief, either premise or derivative, employ one argument at a time until your client has understood the points you are making or you discover that this particular argument is ineffective in some way for him. For example, you might target your client's awfulizing belief about the end of a relationship by using reality-testing arguments, e.g. 'It's the end of the relationship, but does the objective evidence point to the end of your world?' When the client confirms that his awfulizing is unrealistic, use, one at a time, logical and pragmatic arguments on the awfulizing belief. Then use the same three arguments, again, one at a time, for the premise belief (e.g. 'The relationship absolutely should not have ended'). If you have disorder in disputing, you are likely to be jumping from one argument to another and one belief to another, almost certainly confusing your client as well as yourself:

Trainee: Is it correct logic to say that losing your job makes you no good?

[A logical argument targeting self-depreciation.]

Client: It feels like it to me.

Trainee: Where's it going to get you demanding that you absolutely shouldn't have lost your job?

[A pragmatic argument targeting an absolute should.]

Client: Well, I shouldn't have lost it.

Trainee: Is it realistic to call yourself no good on the basis of this job loss or on the basis of any problem in life?

[An empirical argument targeting self-depreciation.]

Client: I am no good. I can't see it any other way.

Trainee: Does it logically follow that, because you didn't want to lose your job, therefore you absolutely shouldn't have lost it?

[A logical argument targeting an absolute should.]

Client: Yes, it does logically follow.

[This non-sequential, chaotic form of disputing is pointless and wastes valuable therapy time. The client is being pulled from pillar to post. To make a bad situation worse (but not awful), the trainee is not paying the slightest attention to the client's replies.]

Key Point

Ensure you have order, not disorder, in disputing.

---

74 Arguing instead of disputing

Disputing in REBT means a careful examination of your client's beliefs, both rational and irrational, in order to determine their self-helping or self-defeating nature. REBT therapists do argue with clients, in the sense of advancing arguments for their consideration, but not in the sense of quarrelling, picking a fight or wearing clients down until they 'confess' their irrationality. Disputing does involve verbal persuasion on your part – you know on theoretical grounds that your client's absolute musts and shoulds and extreme derivatives are irrational – but not verbal coercion (e.g. 'You must see things my way'). You may slip into arguing with your clients for some of the following reasons: you have to prove your clinical competence, the client is holding out for too long against your rational arguments, you have to prove how 'wise' you are or you see it as pointless to discuss with clients their reasons for supporting beliefs that are so patently irrational. In this dialogue, the trainee gets into a heated exchange with her client:

Trainee: Look, no matter what you do, you're never a failure as a person. We've been over this time and time again. When is it going to sink in?

[Alternative response: 'Can you explain again, because I may not have properly understood you, why you think your actions define you as a person?']

Client: That's how I judge myself and others: on the basis of what you do.

Trainee: It's ridiculous to give yourself a global rating on the basis of your actions, whether good or bad. It's self-evident that we are more than our actions. Why can't you see that? What's the point of coming to therapy, if you're not prepared to see things differently?

[Alternative response: 'Would you judge your children as failures, if one of them, for example, failed her exams?']

Client: I do want help with my problems, but I just can't throw my ideas into the dustbin because of your say-so.

Trainee: What do you think I'm talking – rubbish? The 'R' in REBT stands for 'rational thinking', which is what I'm trying to teach you. The very fact you're not being receptive shows how rigid your thinking is.

[Alternative response: 'Which ideas are giving you problems and you wish to target for change or, at least, discussion?' It is evident that the trainee is the rigid thinker. Rational thinking is what makes sense to us, and this varies from person to person. REBT is not the ultimate judge of what is rational or irrational in the world.]

REBT offers clients new ways of understanding and tackling their problems. This usually involves a healthy debate about the pros and cons of change. If you believe you *have* to convince the client of the correctness of your viewpoint, debate disappears and is replaced by arguing and power struggles. Clients are more likely to be convinced by the quality of your arguments and less likely through arguing (see the chapter entitled 'The Best Rational Arguments' in Hauck, 1980).

Key Point

Engage in debate with your clients; avoid arguing with them.

---

75 Disputing inferences while thinking you are disputing beliefs

When you make inferences, you draw conclusions from your observations (e.g. your partner comes home late from work several nights in a row, and you infer she is having an affair, which you are upset about). Inferences can be seen as partially evaluative in nature because they imply an appraisal of a situation (a negative one in the above example). However, REBT views beliefs as the main cognitive determinants of our emotional responses, because they are fully evaluative in nature (e.g. 'My partner must not be having an affair. If he is, that would be awful'); beliefs are evaluations of our inferences. It is crucial to make this distinction between inferences and beliefs because some trainees dispute inferences thinking they are beliefs, thereby leaving intact their clients' disturbance-inducing thinking:

Trainee: Now, your irrational belief is that other people find you boring. Is that right?

[The irrational belief would be something like: 'They must not find me boring because, if they do, this will prove I am a boring person.']

Client: Yes, that's what really worries me.

[Other people might well find her boring, but what's her evaluation of their evaluation?]

Trainee: Now, let's ask whether there is any evidence for this belief?

[The evidence the trainee should be looking for is: where is it written that others must not find her boring, and, if they do, how does that make her a boring person?]

Client: Well, some of my phone calls are not returned or some of my friends seem to hurry by when they see me.

Trainee: That could be true, and I'm not discounting it, but could there be other, more innocent, explanations for their behaviour?

[Finding alternative, more benign responses to negative inferences can help clients to feel better in the short-term, but challenging and changing disturbance-inducing beliefs helps clients to get better in the long-term.]

You might fall into the same trap when you think you are disputing rational beliefs (e.g. 'I would prefer other people not to find me boring, but there is no reason why they must not find me boring'), but, in fact, you are targeting a positive inference for examination (e.g. *Client*: I think that people find me likeable rather than boring after all; *Trainee*: What evidence do you have that people find you likeable rather than boring?).

Key Point

Learn to distinguish inferences from beliefs, and dispute the latter, not the former.

---

76 Misusing vivid disputing methods

Vivid disputing methods are lively, dramatic or memorable ways of disputing irrational beliefs. Two vivid disputing methods are using humour and enactments. Ellis (1977) has said that emotional disturbance can largely be seen as taking ourselves and life *too* seriously. One way to combat this over-serious approach to life is through the use of humour. Humour is used judiciously to make fun of the client's irrational beliefs, never the client. The irrational belief is highlighted before the humour commences (to make it distinct from the person) and feedback is sought from the client to determine the impact of the intervention (it is important to assess whether your client does possess a sense of humour). Humour is best employed, if appropriate, after a therapeutic relationship has been established. Persons cautions that

> the use of humor may not be a good idea for the patient who is so extremely fragile and vulnerable that he feels ridiculed or criticized by the therapist's humorous or sarcastic remarks (1989: 136).

However, you might believe that humour is always therapeutic and aim for a 'fun-filled hour' with your clients or become so enamoured with your own wit that you are oblivious to its grating effect upon them:

Trainee: (smiling) Now, you said your drinking crept up on you again. Let's see what this actually means in practice (the trainee takes an empty bottle from the table, moves it across the floor, up his body and into his mouth). (laughing) Is that what you mean? You cannot be serious (the client is stony-faced). Do you see what I'm getting at with the humour?

Client: (grimly) Only too well.

Trainee: Good. Humour always helps to lighten the load.

[If the trainee had asked the client what she meant by her reply, he might not have been amused by it: 'You think I'm pathetic for making these stupid excuses for drinking again.' This information would have told the trainee not to use humour again in this stage of therapy or to abandon it altogether.]

Enactment in disputing refers to carrying out actions that vividly illustrate the points you are making. For example, instead of asking a client 'How are you a stupid person for acting stupidly?', the therapist could suddenly fling himself to the floor and start barking like a dog for about 30 seconds, resume his seat and ask the client to comment upon his behaviour. The client is likely to say that the therapist's action was stupid or bizarre. The therapist can then ask whether his stupid behaviour makes him a stupid person to emphasize to the client the distinction between rating our behaviour but not rating ourselves on the basis of our behaviour. While flamboyant actions might seem like a lot of fun, they require caution in deciding whether or not to carry them out.

Some clients want a serious or formal relationship with the therapist or have chosen to see him because he is regarded as an expert in his field. Misusing enactments with these kind of clients can bring therapy to an abrupt end (e.g. 'I came to see someone I thought was an expert but ended up seeing an idiot who thinks he's a dog') because they believe you are trivializing their problems with your 'immature' behaviour. Some trainees plunge into enactments without assessing carefully the client's relationship preferences:

Trainee: (dripping wet) Now I've just tipped a glass of water over my head. Does acting foolishly make me a fool?

Client: (sternly) Yes, it does. I thought I was coming for serious counselling. If I want to see that sort of behaviour, I can watch the clowns at the circus.

Trainee: I'm just trying to make a serious point lightheartedly.

Client: I would very much prefer you to make serious points in a serious manner. Any more of this nonsense and I won't be coming back.

Trainee: I apologize for my behaviour, and it won't happen again. Now, to return to serious REBT . . .

Key Point

Do not consider using vivid methods of disputing until you have assessed your clients' relationship preferences. When you do use these methods, gain immediate feedback from your clients to determine the impact of these methods upon them.

PART V
HOMEWORK ERRORS

77 Not setting or reviewing homework assignments

Homework assignments are an indispensable part of REBT. Homework allows your client to put into daily practice the learning that occurs in the counselling sessions, gives him the opportunity to become more competent and confident in facing his problems, facilitates and accelerates his progress towards becoming his own therapist and enables him to act in ways that support his rational belief and undermine his irrational belief. Burns suggests that 'compliance with self-help assignments may be the most important predictor of therapeutic success' (1989: 545). Homework usually forms the bookends of the therapeutic agenda: reviewing homework is the first item on the agenda, while setting homework is the last. Despite the crucial importance of homework tasks, some trainees forget or avoid negotiating them with the client:

Trainee: We've had a very hectic session covering a lot of ground.

Client: I feel exhausted.

Trainee: Shall we not bother with the homework this week?

Client: That would be a good idea.

The trainee's reluctance to set homework may stem from his approval needs or low frustration tolerance (e.g. 'I'm exhausted too. I can't stand having to make the extra effort to set homework'). Other trainee blocks to homework setting may include the belief that homework equals coercing your client, homework will not make any difference to your client's seemingly intractable problems, and, if your client does not carry out the homework, then this proves you are incompetent (Persons, 1989). However, your problems are likely to hold back your client from learning that what she does outside of therapy sessions is ultimately much more important than what goes on inside of them; so identify, challenge and change your beliefs that interfere with homework setting.

When you do set homework tasks, ensure that you review them at the next session, otherwise you will be conveying to your clients that these tasks are actually unimportant or that you are uninterested in their progress. Therefore, do not be surprised if your clients fail to carry them out. Failing to review homework includes this kind of valueless exchange:

Trainee: Did you do the tasks?

Client: Yes, I did.

Trainee: Helpful?

Client: You could say that.

Trainee: Good. Let's move on then.

Reviewing homework involves extracting the *learning* from whatever has occurred – a 'win–win' formula (setting homework tasks in terms of success or failure is a 'win–lose' formula):

1. Did the client carry out the homework successfully? How was she able to achieve this?
2. Did the client encounter any obstacles, and, if she did, how did she manage to overcome them?
3. The client did a homework task but not the agreed one. Why did she change the task?
4. The homework task was quickly abandoned. What went wrong?
5. The agreed task was not carried out. What prevented the client from carrying it out?

Reviewing homework teaches the client how to do it as part of her developing role as a self-therapist.

Key Point

Ensure that you set and review homework tasks in every session.

78 Not making the homework task therapeutically potent

If clients want to ingrain their new rational beliefs and attenuate their old irrational beliefs, then it is important for them to enter and stay in situations that they disturb themselves about. By thinking rationally in these situations, clients can learn to undisturb themselves and thereby re-evaluate the 'horror' with which they previously viewed these situations. Moving too slowly through a hierarchy of feared situations can reinforce a client's fears (e.g. 'I have to go this slow because I can't stand the discomfort involved in moving any faster'), while entering the most feared situation straightaway can be too intense for him and he terminates therapy because he is not ready for 'flooding' (implosion). I (WD) have suggested a middle way between gradualism and flooding called 'challenging, but not overwhelming', i.e. tasks that are sufficiently stimulating to promote therapeutic change but not so daunting that they will inhibit clients from carrying them out. In this dialogue, the trainee negotiates a homework task that is hardly likely to 'stretch' the client:

Trainee: You said that clearing out the spare room is mind-numbingly boring, but you need to get it done.

Client: That's true, but I can't stand boring tasks.

Trainee: How about just doing ten minutes?

Client: I think I can just about manage that. Any longer and I'll start losing my temper and throwing things around.

This homework is likely to strengthen the client's low frustration tolerance beliefs ('I can't stand boring tasks') rather than attack them, as the therapist explains:

Therapist: Can you see any problems with only ten minutes?

Client: That's all I can stand.

Therapist: So, what's the message you will be repeating to yourself, if you go beyond ten minutes?

Client: I can't stand it.

Therapist: Exactly. And that message won't help you clear out the spare room quickly. How many ten-minute efforts will it take you to clear out the room?

Client: Too many. I'll probably give up.

Therapist: What I suggest you do is start clearing out the spare room and stay with your disturbed thoughts and feelings until they subside. How long might that take?

Client: Could be an hour or longer before that happens.

Therapist: What might you learn after an hour?

Client: That I can stand it after all, and I'll get the job done instead of giving up.

Therapist: That's right. You can stand doing boring tasks without liking them. Do you agree to one hour?

Client: One hour it is.

If homework tasks are not therapeutically potent, your clients are likely to be rendered impotent in tackling their problems.

Key Point

Negotiate with your clients challenging, but not overwhelming homework assignments.

79 Not negotiating a homework task that is relevant to the work done in the session

Clients are more likely to carry out their homework when they see the link between the session work, the homework task that logically flows from it and how the homework will help them to reach their goals. In this dialogue, the client is mystified by the homework suggested by the trainee:

Client: We've been talking about my fear of being disliked; so I always try to say and do the right thing. I want to stop doing that and feel okay about saying or doing what I really want to. So I don't understand why you want me to write a short essay on 'Nothing is awful in life'.

Trainee: Sort of help you to see that it isn't the end of your world if people dislike you. Puts things into perspective for you.

Client: My problem is that I can't accept myself if others dislike me. That's what I want help with. I know it isn't the end of my world if I am disliked. So, do I have to do this homework?

[The client's belief is one of self-depreciation, not awfulizing; therefore, tasks involving learning self-acceptance are the relevant ones for the trainee to suggest to the client, like saying things that might displease others and incur criticism or rejection.]

If your clients cannot see, explain or agree with the session – homework–goal link you have suggested, then think again about the clinical relevance of the proposed assignment.

Key Point

Only negotiate homework tasks that are relevant to the work done in each session.

80 Not taking clients through the specifics of homework setting

When your client agrees to carry out a suitable homework task, you might believe that homework negotiation is now over (after all, what else is there to say?). However, carrying out the agreed task remains rather vague (e.g. 'I'll get round to it sometime next week') and can mean that the client will forget to do it, or will do it if nothing more interesting intervenes at the time – the task is not at the forefront of his mind. If you allow homework to be set in this hazy manner, do not be surprised if the client tells you at the next session that he has not done it. In the following dialogue, the therapist concentrates her client's mind on specificity:

Therapist: You've agreed to carry out rational-emotive imagery whereby you want to move from anger to annoyance when you think about your boss's rudeness. Is that right?

Client: That's right. I want to be able to stop seething about it and start being assertive with him.

Therapist: Now, we've practised the imagery in the session; now, when will you practise it in the following week?

Client: Every day.

Therapist: Where will you do it?

Client: At home in the evenings and at work in my lunch break.

Therapist: How often will you do it?

Client: Twice at work and twice in the evening.

Therapist: Any potential or actual obstacles to carrying out the imagery?

[This phase of homework setting is known as troubleshooting.]

Client: I might forget because I am a busy person.

Therapist: What will help you not to forget?

Client: I could write REI [Rational-Emotive Imagery] in my diary for work and stick a Post-it Note on my desk in the study at home.

Therapist: I presume you look in your diary and sit at or go to your study desk every day?

Client: Without fail.

Therapist: Any other obstacles?

Client: None that I can think of.

Therapist: But, if a new obstacle does occur . . . ?

Client: Do the problem solving we've just done.

Specificity, not vagueness, should guide homework negotiation which thereby makes it more likely that your client will commit himself to executing the task. One final point: write down the homework task and give a copy of it to your client, as this will remind him of what he has agreed to do and avoids the potential disagreements at the next session that might arise from a purely verbal agreement:

Client: You said I was to do it twice a week.

Trainee: No, I didn't. I distinctly remember saying twice daily.

Key Point

Be specific in negotiating homework, and troubleshoot obstacles to homework completion.

81 Not encouraging your clients to use force and energy in executing their homework assignments

Ellis (1979) has written about the importance of using force and energy to uproot clients' disturbance-creating beliefs. Clients frequently cling to their irrational thinking with great tenacity and tepid, milk-and-water methods are usually ineffective to uproot such disturbed thinking (e.g. gentle self-affirmations like 'I am a worthwhile human being'). Using force and energy in self-disputing of irrational beliefs can powerfully convince clients that what was previously perceived as unbearable by them is actually bearable, while acting in a way that supports the new rational belief. For example, a client who is tempted to start smoking again tells herself, 'I desperately want a cigarette *but I don't damn well need what I desperately want*' and refuses the offer of a cigarette. She stays in the presence of people smoking in order to teach herself that she does not have to disturb herself about seeing others enjoying a pleasure she has chosen to deprive herself of.

Using force and energy helps clients to move from intellectual to emotional insight into their problems (see Point 60); in other words, they have conviction in their rational beliefs because their effectiveness has been demonstrated in a particular or range of problem areas. In this dialogue, the trainee encourages feebleness and enervation in the client's practice of her rational statements:

Trainee: So, you are going to actively court discomfort by placing a cream cake in front of you and not eating it to prove that you can keep to your diet. Now, what will you say to yourself in order not to eat it?

Client: (weakly) I would prefer to have it, but I'm not going to have it. I hope that will stop me.

Trainee: That might do the trick. See how you get on. Do you want to write that statement down so you remember it at the time when that juicy cream cake is staring you in the face?

Client: No. I think I'll remember it.

[The trainee could have had some cream cakes in the session and helped the client to rehearse using her coping statements with force and energy in order to resist temptation, e.g. 'That cream cake can stay there until it rots. I'M NOT EATING IT!' As it is, she is likely to succumb to temptation in the actual situation.]

Key Point

Teach your clients to use force and energy in carrying out their homework tasks.

---

82 Not using multimodal methods of change

Multimodal disputing involves using cognitive (e.g. rehearsing rational-coping statements), imaginal (e.g. rational-emotive imagery), behavioural (e.g. staying in aversive situations) and emotive (e.g. shame-attacking exercises) methods to promote constructive change. Disputing irrational beliefs multimodally increases the likelihood of removing disturbance-inducing thinking and internalizing a rational outlook. Also, attacking an irrational belief on several fronts can make therapy more interesting for clients rather than advancing on a single front. In this dialogue, the client is uninspired by unimodal attempts at change:

Trainee: You're reading the self-help books and rehearsing your rational-coping statements. How are you getting on?

Client: Nothing seems to be happening.

Trainee: Aren't you learning rational thinking from the books? Maybe your coping statements need looking at again.

Client: All this reading and thinking is a bit of a drag. It's like being back at school again.

Trainee: Well, change is often a slog, but the results are usually worth it.

Client: Hmm.

The client is in danger of being bored to death by the trainee's preoccupation with only cognitive methods of change. The therapist rectifies this in the following exchange:

Therapist: You say the 'reading and thinking is a bit of a drag'. What would liven things up for you?

Client: Some doing, some action.

Therapist: Such as . . . ?

Client: Stop being treated by some of my friends as a taxi: 'Can you take me here, can you take me there?' The next time it happens, I want to say 'no'.

Therapist: And the coping statement behind saying 'no'. . . ?

[The client still needs to have rational ideas underpinning her eagerness for 'some action'.]

Client: 'If you no longer like me because of it, *too bad*.' That gets the juices flowing. I want to start practising self-acceptance, not just keep reading about it.

[For a discussion of multimodal methods of change, see, for example, Walen et al., 1992.]

Key Point

Use multimodal methods of change to help your clients overcome their emotional problems.

83 Not checking whether your client has the skills to execute the homework task

You might assume that, if your client has agreed to the homework task, then he has the skills to carry it out. However, he might have agreed to carry it out without thinking through what will be actually required of him, and you may have overlooked this important point too. Overlooking skills assessment can mean homework failure:

Client: I didn't do the homework. I'm not ready to start socializing again. I don't know what to say or how to behave socially. I'm out of practice after my long illness.

Trainee: Why didn't you mention this when we were discussing homework at the end of the last session?

Client: You didn't ask me.

Trainee: Oh.

This client will probably need a lot of in-session social-skills-building practice before venturing into social situations. In the following dialogue, the therapist teases out the client's level of skill with regard to being assertive with her overbearing partner:

Therapist: So, when your partner starts bossing you around, you are going to act assertively towards him. Is that right?

Client: That's right. I'm going to lay into that bastard and give him hell.

Therapist: That sounds like anger rather than assertion. What is likely to happen if you 'lay into that bastard', as you call him?

Client: We'll probably end up throwing things at each other or worse.

Therapist: Now, assertion means standing up for yourself without anger. Do you want to be genuinely assertive with him or angry with him?

Client: I think I'll try the assertion first.

Therapist: I suggest some skills practice in the session before you try it out with him. How does that sound?

Client: Okay. What do we do, then?

Key Point

Check that your client has the skills to execute her homework tasks; if she does not possess these skills, then you will need to teach them.

---

84 Accepting 'trying' instead of focusing on 'doing'

Clients frequently say they will try to carry out their homework. This seems at first glance a perfectly reasonable reply. What else would you expect them to say? However, while trying suggests they will make an effort, it also denotes a lack of commitment on their part because they have not yet grasped the philosophical implications of what real change actually requires from them: forceful and persistent action, not half-hearted attempts at it. In our experience, many trainees let an 'I'll try' reply go unexplored, which the therapist does not do in this exchange:

Therapist: When you say 'I'll try to do the homework', what do you mean by that?

Client: I'll do my best, I'll try. That's what I mean.

Therapist: How long have you been trying to overcome this problem?

Client: About ten years.

Therapist: Where has this attitude got you with overcoming your problem?

Client: Not far.

Therapist: So, if you continue to try, you are hardly likely to make much progress or, more likely, stay as you are with your anxiety problems. Now, when this session is over, will you leave the room or try to? Will you drive home or try to?

Client: I will leave the room; I will drive home.

Therapist: What's the point I'm making?

Client: Doing gets it done, trying doesn't.

Therapist: To really drive home this point, for homework, do you want to note down every day what you actually do and what you try to do?

Client: I think that would be very useful to get this difference clear in my mind.

Therapist: (smiles) At the next session, we'll review whether you did the task or tried to.

Key Point

Discuss with your clients the differences between a trying and doing outlook in effecting constructive change.

---

85 Rushing homework negotiation

We have emphasized the vital importance of homework tasks in Point 78 but many trainees rush homework negotiation because they leave it to the last minute or two of the session. This usually means that the homework task is dictated by the trainee or high-speed negotiation results in confusion for the client:

Trainee: (talking quickly) We've only got a couple of minutes left of the session. This is what you need to do for homework: really get stuck into that irrational belief of yours, all right?

Client: What's my irrational belief, and what do I have to get 'stuck into'?

Trainee: What we discussed. So, good luck with the homework.

Client: I'll need it.

It would be a great surprise if the client did the homework as he does not know what it is. Ensure that you make provision for homework negotiation in the structure of the session (it is a key agenda item) – ten minutes or even longer for novice REBTers. If a homework task has emerged earlier in the session and been agreed upon, then you will still need several minutes at the end of the session to remind the client of what he has agreed to do. We would suggest that you practise homework negotiation with your fellow trainees, incorporating all the points made in this section of the book, and time how long it takes. This exercise should help you to see that homework negotiation usually takes longer that you anticipate it will.

> ## Key Point
>
> Do not rush homework negotiation; if you do, it is less likely that your client will carry out the task or carry it out successfully.

86 Not capitalizing on successful homework completion

The obvious procedure to follow when clients fail to execute homework tasks successfully is to discover what happened. What is much less obvious to many trainees is *capitalizing* on successful homework completion:

Trainee: Did you get into the lift and go up two floors?

Client: I did, and it wasn't as bad as I thought. Actually, I could have gone all the way to the top, but that wasn't the agreed homework. It would have been great to do it, though.

Trainee: You don't want to start rushing things, just take it steady. A couple of floors at a time will be sufficient.

The trainee's caution may be based on his fear that a faster rate of progress could lead to disaster (e.g. the client suffers a severe panic attack in the lift and an ambulance is called), and he will be blamed for it, or the trainee does not know how to react adaptively to changing clinical circumstances, preferring to 'stick to our agreed plan of action'. In the next dialogue, the therapist seeks to capitalize on the client's enthusiasm for faster progress:

Therapist: When we first discussed the strategy for overcoming your fear of lifts, we agreed that it would be slow and gradual. It sounds like you want to change that now. Correct?

Client: Yes, I do. I want to go all the way to the top floor in one go. I want that to be the next homework task.

Therapist: Agreed. Now, if you couldn't get to the top in one go . . . ?

Client: I wouldn't be upset or despairing. I just know that I can do more to overcome this problem than I'm currently doing, and I want to get on with it.

Therapist: That's fine.

Key Point

Capitalize on your clients' successful homework completion and their desire to quicken the pace of change.

PART VI:
WORKING-THROUGH ERRORS

87 Not eliciting and responding to your clients' doubts about or objections to REBT

It is probable that many of your clients will have doubts about or objections to REBT. If these doubts and objections remain unaddressed, then these clients are likely to be influenced by them to the detriment of their own therapeutic progress in internalizing a rational outlook. These doubts and objections can involve any aspect of REBT. Some trainees believe that clients' understanding of a particular REBT concept is the same as agreeing with it and therefore do not elicit from their clients any reservations they may have:

Client: So, high frustration tolerance is about learning to endure: put up with things without having to like them.

Trainee: That's right. Now, let's focus on disputing those irrational beliefs that block you from achieving high frustration tolerance, or HFT for short.

Does the client have any objections to learning HFT? This question is asked by the therapist and the client responds in the following way:

Client: Actually, I do. If I'm just supposed to put up with everything, then my life will be an endless struggle: just grin and bear it. I'm not excited by that prospect at all. I might as well give up therapy now.

Therapist: Thank you for that feedback. HFT is not meant to be a life of grim endurance but learning to tolerate those things that you currently believe are intolerable in order to reach your goals. So, learning HFT is directly related to helping you to achieve your goals.

[The therapist responds to the client's objections non-defensively and corrects her misconceptions about HFT.]

Client: So, HFT would help me to get on with this immensely boring paperwork thereby meeting my deadlines – which is my goal – instead of missing them. Is that right?

Therapist: Correct. Do you want to see how to put HFT into practice?

Client: Now that we've cleared things up, yes, I do.

Some clients have serious doubts about moving from intellectual to emotional insight into their problems (i.e. believing their new rational beliefs deeply instead of lightly) because of the cost to them of surrendering their irrational beliefs. As Rorer explains:

> When confronted with a client who accepts the therapist's argument, but who nevertheless cannot give up an irrational belief, it is important to ask what it would mean to the client to give up the belief. In general, we do not hold any belief in a vacuum, so we may not be able to modify or give up a belief without modifying or giving up other related beliefs that may be important to us because they involve our self-image, our world view, or our deepest fears. It is the changes in these other beliefs, and what the client thinks the consequences of making those changes would be, that I refer to as the cost of giving up the irrational belief (1999: 224-5).

If you do not examine the client's wider belief system within which his irrational belief is embedded, then disputing the belief will probably be ineffective because it is held 'in check' by this system. In this excerpt, the therapist elicits from the client why he believes he cannot surrender his irrational belief:

Therapist: What would it cost you, if you give up your belief 'I must never show weakness'?

Client: Well, that would strike at the heart of my self-image and the way I've conducted myself and my life all these years. Giving up the belief means I would become weak, not be strong any more.

Therapist: So, all the values and beliefs you've followed all these years would come tumbling down. Is that right?

Client: That's what could happen.

Therapist: Would things come tumbling down if you made a crucial distinction between acknowledging a weakness but not condemning yourself for having it or seeing that a particular weakness does not sum up your whole character?

Client: It just seems you want me to repudiate my past behaviour, as if I've got everything wrong all my life.

Therapist: I certainly don't want you to do that or think that, but, instead, look at the possibility of learning from past experiences, not repudiating them, in order to develop a more flexible and compassionate response to yourself, when things go wrong in your life. To make adjustments to your beliefs, certainly not discard them.

Client: (sighs deeply) I can be compassionate to others, when they show weaknesses, but not to myself. I know up here (tapping head) that what you say makes sense, but it's such a big step to take.

Therapist: Can we discuss further this 'big step'?

Client: I'm willing to do that at least.

Clients' reluctance to move from intellectual to emotional insight can be very difficult to resolve, and we offer no glib solutions to this problem. However, what often does encourage clients to work at adopting a rational belief to counter the irrational one is the quality of your arguments and your patience in presenting them and responding to your clients' doubts about them. Encouraging your clients to express their doubts shows them that their views are taken seriously by you and that they are not expected to absorb REBT passively.

Key Point

Remember that your clients will have doubts about and objections to REBT; so elicit and respond to them in a non-defensive manner. Unaddressed doubts and objections are likely to hinder or derail your clients' progress.

88 Not helping your clients to become self-therapists in the working-through phase of REBT

Working through is defined by Grieger and Boyd as:

> Helping clients work through their problems – that is, systematically giving up their irrational ideas – is where most of the therapist's energy and time are directed and where long-lasting change takes place. Successful working through leads to significant change, whereas unsuccessful working through leads to no gain or to superficial gain at best. It is as simple as that (1980: 122).

The ultimate aim of REBT is for clients to become their own therapists for both present and future emotional and practical problem-solving. Encouraging your clients to become self-therapists is promoted by you in transferring to them increasing responsibility for analysing and tackling their problems within the ABCDE model. This means them becoming more verbally active in the sessions and taking the lead in identifying, assessing and dealing with their problems and, correspondingly, you becoming less active-directive while still keeping your clients on track. For example, using prompts (i.e. short, focused questions) instead of explanations 'nudges' your client through describing an emotional episode in ABC terms and designing a relevant homework task. However, many trainees still 'take charge' of problem-solving in the working-through phase, thereby inhibiting clients from learning what self-therapy means:

Client: I got anxious again yesterday when my boss asked to see me.

Trainee: Okay, you've got asked to see your boss at A, you are feeling anxious at C, then you are making a demand at B about A, which leads to C. What is the 'must' you are telling yourself?

If the trainee does not allow the client to work things out for himself, his gains from therapy will probably not be maintained in the long-term. In this dialogue, the therapist stands back and 'lets the client's brain take the strain' of problem assessment:

Therapist: How do we make ABC sense of this problem?

Client: Well, C is obviously my anxiety. Being asked to see my boss is the A.

Therapist: Do you remember how to identify what you are most disturbed or anxious about?

Client: (thinking hard) Follow through in my mind what the situation means to me, so he wants to see me then . . . er . . . he will comment upon my work . . .

Therapist: In what way will he comment on it?

Client: Oh, unfavourably. Right, he will criticize my work, and, if he does, this will mean . . . I'm incompetent. I found it – the irrational belief.

Therapist: Is that the whole belief?

Client: Er . . . let me see . . . the must is missing. Right, the whole belief is 'He must not criticize my work because, if he does, this will mean I'm incompetent'. That wasn't too difficult, after all.

Therapist: The more you practise these skills both in and out of the sessions, the quicker you will become your own therapist or problem-solver.

The therapist then asks her client what questions would help him to dispute his irrational belief and what homework task would he design to challenge his belief in the workplace (the therapist would provide prompts if the client had difficulty answering these questions). As your clients take over the reins of therapy, you can reconceptualize your role as a consultant, coach, mentor or adviser rather than as a therapist.

Key Point

At the earliest opportunity in therapy, encourage your clients to start adopting the role of a self-therapist.

89 Not discussing with your clients that change is non-linear

Some clients might assume that, once they start thinking rationally, emotional disturbance will disappear from their lives. Change will be a smooth, pleasant and uneventful process. If you do not elicit and counter such a view with a realistic picture of the change process, setbacks or relapses can come as a great shock:

Client: Someone called me 'stupid' and I just collapsed. Everything fell apart. I've been accepting myself, not paying attention to those sort of comments. Now I've gone back to square one. Thinking rationally is hopeless; it doesn't work. You said self-acceptance would give me emotional stability. You got it completely wrong.

Trainee: Well, I'm sure that I mentioned it wouldn't all be plain sailing.

Client: If you mentioned it, I didn't hear it.

To avoid or minimize such 'shocks', prepare your clients for the vicissitudes of the change process by explaining to them the non-linear model of change:

1. Frequency – are your unhealthy negative emotions and counterproductive behaviours experienced less frequently than before?
2. Intensity – when your unhealthy negative emotions and counterproductive behaviours are experienced, are they less intense than before?
3. Duration – do your unhealthy negative emotions and counterproductive behaviours last for shorter periods than before?

Encourage your clients to keep a log of their unhealthy negative emotions and counterproductive behaviours and the situations in which they occur so they can measure emotional and behavioural change using these three dimensions. This log will help to provide evidence of change when some clients complain that none has occurred. The non-linear model of change underscores Albert Ellis's observation that we can make ourselves less disturbed, but never undisturbable.

Key Point

Discuss the non-linear model of change with your clients to prepare them for the 'rocky road ahead'.

---

90 Not explaining to your clients cognitive-emotive dissonance reactions to the change process

Clients frequently complain of feeling 'unnatural', 'weird' or 'strange' as they work towards attenuating their often deeply held irrational beliefs and internalizing a rational outlook. This phenomenon is often referred to as 'cognitive-emotive dissonance': trying to believe a new rational belief while at the same believing the old irrational belief – 'they [clients] see a better way, but cannot yet actualize it, so they conclude they cannot possibly overcome their disturbance' (Grieger and Boyd, 1980: 161). At this point, some clients are likely to terminate therapy to feel 'natural' again (i.e. return to their self-defeating thinking). Trainees frequently forget to warn clients of these dissonant reactions or explain how to cope with them – something the therapist does not forget to do in this dialogue:

Client: I'm beginning to feel very awkward and strange trying to accept myself, when I've spent so much of my life putting myself down.

Therapist: You're entering a stage in therapy where your old ways of thinking and feeling are in conflict with your new ways of thinking and feeling. This conflict leads to those awkward and strange feelings you're experiencing.

Client: How long will it last?

Therapist: Let's just say for the sake of argument a couple of months, but longer for more deeply ingrained irrational beliefs. It's important to tolerate these feelings until they pass, persist with your disputing when you put yourself down and keep on striving for self-acceptance. This current strange state of yours will eventually change into a more natural and comfortable state, if you keep on practising your rational ideas.

Client: So put up with the strange feelings and persist with the disputing until I get through this uncomfortable stage. That's the message, right?

Therapist: Correct.

Key Point

Prepare your clients for experiencing cognitive-emotive dissonance reactions as they move through the change process, and show them how to cope with these reactions.

---

91 Not discussing with your clients philosophical vs. non-philosophical change

Philosophical change refers to uprooting demands and their derivatives from your thinking. Philosophical change can be situation-specific, cross-situational or influence every area of your life. Non-philosophical change involves challenging inferences rather than the demands from which they are derived, focusing only on behavioural change or avoiding or changing unpleasant activating events instead of facing them (non-philosophical changes are often referred to as compromises in REBT). Whether your client pursues philosophical or non-philosophical change often depends on you discussing these different outcomes with him – something the trainee does not do here:

Client: I'm feeling less anxious now; so I think it's time to leave therapy.

Trainee: So, are you reassured that people do like you?

Client: I am now. I go through these phases when I think I'm unlikeable, panic for a bit that no one likes me, then someone says I'm getting things out of perspective, and I calm down.

Trainee: We'll make this the last session then as you're feeling calmer.

The client would be leaving therapy feeling better but not getting better because her disturbance-inducing ideas remain intact (Ellis, 1972). In this dialogue, the therapist discusses the pros and cons of leaving therapy at this point:

Therapist: It's good that you're feeling better, but don't you still believe deep down that you are unlikeable if others do dislike you?

Client: That's true, but what's the point you're making?

Therapist: It's this: the next time someone says they dislike you or you think they do, you'll have another bout of anxiety and panic. If you were to change your outlook from 'I'm unlikeable, if others dislike me' to 'I can accept myself irrespective of how others see me', then this new outlook is likely to be the basis of enduring emotional stability in your life. Your present belief only provides you with temporary emotional stability.

Client: Hmm. I can see what you're getting at, but I'm not sure whether I want to go down that route. It seems like a lot of hard work.

Therapist: I'm certainly not trying to force you to go down that route but presenting some options to you between what I see as short-term versus long-term solutions to your problems.

Client: Let me think about it, and I'll give you my decision in the next session.

Key Point

Ensure that you discuss with your clients the pros and cons of philosophical vs. non-philosophical change.

92 Accepting a client's pseudo-rationality as a genuinely rational outlook

A minority of clients will develop a pseudo-rational outlook which usually interferes with their ability to effect meaningful emotional and behavioural changes in their lives. Such clients

> become avid consumers of rational emotive behavioural books and audiotapes, and make themselves extremely knowledgeable about REBT's theory and practice. They can quote extensively from the REBT literature and are able to give all the 'right' answers to counsellors' disputing questions during sessions, but fail to put their knowledge into practice between sessions (Dryden et al., 1999: 251).

In our experience, it can be difficult for trainees to distinguish between genuine and pseudo-rationality because they are not usually looking for discrepancies between what the client says he believes and what he actually does. In the following dialogue, the therapist is troubled by the client's professed rationality:

Therapist: Your goal was to ask women out, but what stopped you was a fear of rejection leading to self-rejection. Now you've become self-accepting, you say you don't need to ask women out. I don't understand.

Client: Now that I'm self-accepting, I no longer fear rejection; so I don't need to ask women out to prove to myself what I now believe.

Therapist: Surely the real test of belief change is putting yourself in the line of fire – in your case, to face rejection?

Client: Why bother proving what's self-evident? I am self-accepting.

Therapist: Self-acceptance was a means to an end, not an end in itself. Presumably you can't have much sexual satisfaction from self-acceptance or develop a relationship with a concept. The goal was to ask women out. Have you actually asked any women out?

Client: (quietly) No.

Therapist: Because . . . ?

Client: I'm still scared of being rejected.

Therapist: Shall we work towards genuine self-acceptance and asking women out? Rationality with results.

Client: Yes. Being alone is no fun.

Key Point

Be on the alert for discrepancies between your clients' professed rationality and what a genuinely rational outlook entails.

93 Not helping your clients to generalize their learning to other problematic situations in their lives

An important way of helping your client to maintain his therapeutic gains is by encouraging him to generalize his REBT learning from problems he has tackled successfully to other areas in his life. For example, if your client has overcome his low frustration tolerance about meeting deadlines at work, he can then transfer what he has learnt to other LFT-related situations in his life, such as impatience in traffic jams or long queues. Spreading the effects of change in this way is overlooked by the trainee in this exchange:

Trainee: So, you are now able to say 'no' when one or two people at work try to dump some of their work on you?

Client: That's right. At least that's that problem sorted out.

Trainee: If you've got other problems as well, just use REBT in the same way. Okay?

[The trainee assumes that the client can automatically transfer this learning to other situations in his life.]

Client: (frowning) Hmm.

[The client does not sound too confident about being able to do this.]

Most of your clients will need help with this generalization process; so build it in to therapy by helping them to carry more of the responsibility for identifying, challenging and changing their irrational beliefs in specific situations and then in a broader range of situations. Ultimately, clients should remember that when they are emotionally disturbed, they will usually have 'sneaked' a rigid must or an absolute should into their thinking, which needs to be detected and disputed.

Key Point

Encourage your clients to generalize their REBT learning by explicitly teaching them how to do it.

94 Not helping your clients to look for core irrational beliefs

Another way of helping your clients to move from dealing with specific problems to more wide-ranging problems is to help them identify, challenge and change core irrational beliefs which are central self-defeating rules of living. These beliefs can be difficult to detect as they remain dormant during periods of stability in our lives. They are usually activated and enter our awareness when we experience emotional distress or unpleasant events. Disputing a situation-specific irrational belief helps clients to deal more effectively with that specific situation, while disputing a core irrational belief usually means a number of adverse situations are tackled simultaneously. Clients who are able to detect and deal with their core irrational beliefs are better placed to extend their REBT learning across a wide number of situations. You might believe that, after you have helped your clients to detect and dispute a few situation-specific irrational beliefs, your 'job is done'. However, situation-specific beliefs can be seen as specific forms of a core belief; therefore, you have only been 'chipping away' at it instead of demolishing it. In this dialogue, the therapist believes there is 'more work to be done', if the client is interested:

Therapist: We've looked at situations where you agonized over a career change, getting out of a dull relationship and changing to a new make of car. Can you see a theme running through these situations?

[Looking for a theme(s) that connects a number of situations is one method of identifying a core irrational belief.]

Client: (musing) A theme. Hmm. I think it's to do with certainty.

Therapist: My hunch is that you say to yourself something like this: 'I must be certain that, if I change things in my life, they must work out well for me, and, if they don't, my life will be awful.' Does that ring any bells?

[The therapist presents her hypothesis for consideration by the client.]

Client: That sounds pretty accurate. That's why it takes me a long time to make my mind up about things.

Therapist: We've discussed three situations that this belief is connected to. Are there any others you are aware of?

Client: Quite a few I can think of and probably more I can't think of at this moment.

Therapist: Do you want to tackle this core belief that extends into other problem areas in your life?

Client: I think I would. I know this agonizing of mine wastes so much time, so much effort, and with virtually nothing positive to show for it.

If you do help your client to identify a core irrational belief, then help him to design a core rational belief to challenge it in every situation that it is operative (e.g. 'I would like to be certain that things work out well for me, but there is no reason why they must work out well for me. If they don't, my life will be made more difficult but not awful'). In our experience, it is unlikely that one core belief underlies all your client's problems; typically, it is at least two or three involving both ego and discomfort disturbance.

Key Point

Make sure that you help your clients to look for their core irrational beliefs. When located, then help your clients to design core rational beliefs to counter them.

95 Not helping your clients to understand how they perpetuate their core irrational beliefs

REBT mainly focuses on how clients maintain their emotional problems rather than on how they were acquired. Core irrational beliefs may have been present since childhood or adolescence and have maintained a powerful 'grip' ever since. As part of REBT's psycho-educational approach, help your clients to understand how they perpetuate their core irrational beliefs. This perpetuation process occurs in three main ways:

1. Maintenance of core irrational beliefs, i.e. thinking and acting in ways that maintain the core belief, e.g. a client who thinks he is a fool behaves in foolish ways to make others laugh, thereby reinforcing his self-image.
2. Avoidance of core irrational beliefs, i.e. the cognitive, emotive and behavioural strategies clients use to avoid activating painful affect, e.g. a client turns to drink to 'blot out' facing the failures in her life, but the act of avoidance just reminds her that 'I am a failure'.
3. Compensation for irrational beliefs, i.e. engaging in actions that appear to contradict the core belief e.g. a client drives himself relentlessly to prove he is competent but this strategy backfires and he 'burns out', confirming in his mind that he is incompetent.

In the following dialogue, the trainee seems as mystified as his client as to why she continues to think and act in self-defeating ways:

Client: No matter what I do, I never seem to think it's good enough; then I think I'm no good. There's no job I won't take on. Others shrink back but not me. Why can't I get over this 'I'm no good' crap?

[It seems the client is striving to compensate for her core belief of 'I'm no good'.]

Trainee: Well, you think that way because you do. That's it really. Just accept it, and then we can challenge it.

Client: It's really important for me to know. I feel I can't move on until I know.

The therapist provides some education about her core belief:

Therapist: How long have you had this core belief?

Client: Since my late teens, I think.

Therapist: What have you been trying to prove since then?

Client: That I am good enough rather than no good.

Therapist: But no matter what you do, what you achieve, you can never shake off that 'I'm no good' belief. Is that right?

Client: That's right.

Therapist: What seems to be happening, then, is that you try to prove to yourself that you are good enough, but, when these attempts fail, you go back to putting yourself down. So your activities help to keep alive your negative self-image. Is that how it works?

Client: Yes, it is. I seem to be like the mouse on the wheel in his cage who's going nowhere. Okay, it's beginning to make sense; so what do I do about it, then?

It is important not only to help your clients understand their own particular ways of perpetuating their core beliefs but also to assist them to develop robust cognitive, behavioural and emotive strategies to halt and then reverse the perpetuation process. With the above client, she can learn self-acceptance (e.g. 'I'm neither good nor bad, just a fallible human being who is no longer going to rate herself, only her behaviour'), reveal to others that she has given up the 'self-rating game' and only select work that is important to her. Finally, she can learn to enjoy herself rather than prove herself.

Key Point

Teach your clients how they perpetuate their core irrational beliefs; then show them how to halt and reverse this perpetuation process.

96 Neglecting the importance of teaching relapse prevention

As therapy draws to an end, REBT focuses on teaching clients relapse-prevention strategies. Relapse prevention helps clients to identify those situations (e.g. negative emotional states, interpersonal strife) that they could disturb themselves about and thereby trigger the re-emergence of their emotional and behavioural difficulties. It is highly likely that lapses will occur, and, if you have not helped your client to anticipate and deal with these lapses, they could easily lead to a relapse followed by him returning to see you believing that his therapeutic gains have been 'wiped out' (or so demoralized by this 'collapse' that he does not contact you). Some trainees avoid discussing relapse prevention because they believe it ends therapy on a pessimistic note:

Supervisor: Why pessimistic instead of realistic?

Trainee: Well, the client has been doing so well, I just think it will dampen her spirits if I mention the possibility of her panic attacks reappearing.

Supervisor: If you don't discuss relapse and they do come back, then what?

Trainee: I suppose she might be overwhelmed by them because I haven't discussed or prepared her for their possible return.

Supervisor: So, do you want to help your client to prepare for the possibility of post-therapy setbacks or just enjoy the feel-good factor of seemingly successful therapy?

Trainee: Okay, I agree. The responsible and self-helping strategy is teaching relapse prevention.

Relapse prevention in REBT will be based on the skills you have already taught your clients and should be an important part of your treatment plan as 'outcome is increasingly measured not only by treatment success but by relapse prevention' (Padesky and Greenberger, 1995: 70).

Key Point

Do not forget the importance of teaching relapse-prevention strategies.

---

97 Not encouraging self-actualization when the client indicates it as a goal

Self-actualization is defined as 'realizing one's potential; the continuing process of actualising or putting into practice one's aspirations rather than ignoring, denying or suppressing them' (Feltham and Dryden, 1993: 170). REBT teaches clients not only to overcome their emotional problems but also to pursue self-actualization if they want a more fulfilling life (Ellis, 1994). Once your clients have overcome their presenting difficulties by internalizing a rational outlook, you can then discuss some of the goals that would bring them greater happiness in life. However, some trainees think that, once clients' emotional problems are overcome, it is time to end therapy:

Client: You know, now that I'm not ranting and raving at work any more, I really am fed up with office politics: all the backstabbing – in fact, working for other people. My dream is to be self-employed.

Trainee: Oh, good luck with that. Anyway, shall we arrange a follow-up appointment to see how you're getting on?

Client: Can do.

In this dialogue, the therapist discusses the client's yearning to be self-employed:

Therapist: Do you intend to follow your dream?

Client: I've already handed in my notice. I'd be interested in your opinion.

Therapist: I think, where it's possible, people should fulfil their dreams. I would urge you to remember to problem-solve rationally when you encounter obstacles to becoming self-employed.

Client: I know it won't be easy, and I'll remember my REBT learning, but I'm determined to give it a go.

Therapist: That's great to hear. One further point: when you do become self-employed, that won't be the end of the dream, so to speak, but will present new challenges and experiences for you. So it's important to have an open mind about what leading a happier life can involve as opposed to having a fixed view about what it must involve.

Client: I realize I need to be open-minded about what lies ahead, but what lies ahead will, I'm sure, be much more interesting and fulfilling than what I'm leaving behind.

[The therapist should encourage the client to keep in contact, though with less frequent sessions, in order to monitor his progress towards his self-actualization goals.]

Key Point

Some clients will want to think beyond their emotional goals and discuss their aspirations for a happier life. Be alert to and engage in this kind of discussion.

PART VII
SELF-MAINTENANCE ERRORS

98 Not looking after yourself

You might spend so much time helping others that you neglect looking after your own physical and mental welfare. For example, you do not undertake regular exercise, become a workaholic, drink and eat excessively, your sense of humour disappears and your IQ (irritability quotient: Burns, 1981) rises sharply. In this extract, the supervisor comments on the trainee's irritable manner:

Supervisor: In your tapes, you are sharp and impatient with your clients as if they are irritating you because they don't get to the point.

Trainee: Well, I've got so many clients to see and they're always rambling on, so many books to read, essays to write, supervision to attend. It's always pressure. I never get a moment's peace.

Supervisor: What do you think will happen if you continue not to 'get a moment's peace'?

Trainee: The dreaded burn-out. I feel it's already on its way.

Supervisor: What good will you be to yourself, clients, family, friends, partner and so on, if you burn out?

Trainee: I'll just be one sad, miserable git.

Supervisor: Do you want to get some balance back into your life? Learn how to pace yourself for the long-term instead of running yourself into the ground?

Trainee: What do I have to do?

Supervisor: What if I were to refer you to an REBT therapist?

Trainee: Well, I'm definitely not applying it to myself; so I suppose I do need some help. Okay.

A not-so-obvious form of self-neglect is not accepting your temperamental tendencies, and, instead, condemning yourself for them. For example, I (MN) have LFT towards anything mechanical when it breaks down. I demand it should be instantly fixed rather than have to work out the solution for myself (I see myself as a 'useless bastard' for not having the patience to work it out). I doubt whether I will ever see the day when this response is entirely gone from my life. As Dryden and Yankura observe:

> We hold that you will take more care of yourself if you identify your temperamentally based patterns and accept yourself for them. You can certainly work to curb the excesses of these patterns, but if you accept the fact that you will not be able to change the 'pull' of your temperament, you will relax and even celebrate your temperament as being part of your uniqueness (1995: 128).

Also with regard to your temperament, find a job profile that suits it rather than goes against its grain. For example, I (WD) enjoy pursuing the 'life of the mind' through writing, teaching and researching in an academic setting, whereas working in a retail setting selling washing machines or television sets would be for me 'lifeless and mindless'.

Finally, strive to be authentic with yourself and others. By being authentic with yourself, we mean not trying to convince yourself that you are other than you are, accepting your faults and limitations without despair and seeking to address them in a constructive way. Being authentic with others means allowing them to see your real self rather than a simulated self – the latter 'self' is often employed if you believe you need others' approval or you want to hide your true feelings from them. Authenticity with self and others rests on self-acceptance – a key REBT principle for the maintenance of mental health.

Key Point

Be the guardian of your own physical and mental wellbeing in order to maximize your happiness and minimize your unhappiness.

99 Disturbing yourself about your clients' disturbances

While concern and compassion are important qualities to display to your clients as they relate their problems to you, being too concerned and desperate to 'heal the client's pain' can lead you to becoming just as disturbed as your clients. At this point, your clinical competence will probably start to decline as you become more and more absorbed in your anguish:

Supervisor: How will your suffering for her lessen her own suffering?

Trainee: She's been through so much, more than any human being should have to bear. It's just so unfair: one tragedy after another.

Supervisor: She's had a lot of harrowing experiences, but you didn't answer my question: how will your suffering reduce hers?

Trainee: At least it shows I care, but, no, my suffering has made no impact on hers.

Supervisor: When you say 'at least it shows I care', it seems to me you are confusing caring, which is a compassionate response to a distressed individual, with caring too much, which involves you becoming disturbed about their distress.

Trainee: I think you're right; I have crossed the line into caring too much.

Supervisor: So, shouldn't you be helping her to bear the unbearable rather than showing her, through your behaviour, that her problems are unbearable?

Trainee: I'm sure that's what I'm doing; it's important to stay focused on her problems, not mine.

Supervisor: One other thing: when she goes out and your next client comes in, where's your attention?

Trainee: Still with her and not on the client sitting in front of me; so I'm not helping this client either.

Supervisor: If you lose your objectivity and allow yourself to be sucked into the client's problems, you don't help her and the next client and your skills go out the window. Is that your goal as a therapist?

Trainee: Of course not. In my next session tape, I hope to show you that I've regained my clinical focus and composure.

Pitying clients, or despairing over how life or others have treated them, is best handled if you accept

> the rational idea that *one does not have to be disturbed over other people's problems and disturbances*. Get hold of that idea securely, think it through in great depth, and accept it as a wonderfully sane piece of advice . . . Stop pitying people and you will bring yourself back on the right track (Hauck, 1980: 238–9; original author's italics).

Key Point

Learn not to disturb yourself about your clients' disturbances, thereby staying clinically focused on their problems rather than distracted or absorbed by your own.

100 Sacredizing REBT

Sacredizing REBT refers to treating it as a form of religiosity. Ellis describes religiosity as

> a devout or rigid belief in some kind of secular religion (such as Libertarianism, Marxism, or Freudianism) – that is, a dogmatic, absolutistic conviction that some political, economic, social, philosophic view is sacrosanct, provides ultimate answers to virtually all important questions, and is to be piously subscribed to and followed by everyone who wishes to lead a good life (1983: 1).

To sacredize REBT is to stop practising it, i.e. REBT's open-minded approach to knowledge is transformed by you into a rigid conviction that REBT is the supreme and unquestioned source of all knowledge for understanding and tackling our problems in life – you become close-minded in other words. If you adopt this dogmatic standpoint, you are likely to experience the following blind spots:

1. You will not see or look for any weaknesses in REBT theory or practice.
2. You will not listen to or summarily dismiss criticism of REBT.
3. Your evangelical zeal will probably 'scare off' some clients, while others are viewed by you as inadequate or lacking 'real' commitment to change because they do not 'work hard enough' to embrace REBT as wholeheartedly as you have done.
4. You make yourself emotionally disturbed more easily (e.g. angry) when other therapists or some clients attack REBT, or friends and family poke fun at you when you try to teach it to them.
5. You start losing your sense of humour as fervour replaces fun in your sessions (when the previous use of humour was therapeutically appropriate).

In the following dialogue, the supervisor points out the trainee's rigid practice of REBT:

Supervisor: In your session tape, you've told the client on several occasions that she must think rationally. Doesn't REBT want to remove musturbatory thinking, not encourage it?

Trainee: She has to get better, though.

Supervisor: How will that happen, if, through your teaching, she replaces one irrational belief with another?

Trainee: But she's got to see that rational thinking will solve her emotional problems.

Supervisor: Why has she got to see it? Why can't you present the options to her and allow her to make up her own mind?

Trainee: What's the point of teaching REBT if the client doesn't use it?

Supervisor: But that's her choice. Do you want to deprive her of freedom of choice, freedom of thought?

Trainee: Of course not, but she should see that REBT will help her. She keeps on resisting.

[The unspoken part of the trainee's last sentence is probably '. . . as she absolutely shouldn't do'. Given the trainee's train of thought, 'she should see . . .' is highly likely to be absolute too. With regard to his warped practice of REBT, the trainee is a dedicated dogmatist.]

Supervisor: Look, the bottom line is this: you're practising REBT in a rigid way, which goes against the teaching of REBT. In other words, you've made yourself a non-REBTer. Do you want to practise REBT in its proper and flexible way or remain preaching dogmatism?

Trainee: Well, I suppose start seeing the error of my ways.

Supervisor: And you can start that by reading the first three chapters of *A Practitioner's Guide to Rational-Emotive Therapy* [Walen et al., 1992] to reacquaint yourself with REBT as Ellis conceived it, and we'll discuss what you have learnt from your reading at our next session. Okay?

Trainee: Okay.

Key Point

Do not adopt an uncritical adherence to REBT. Keep your critical faculties sharp and sceptical.

101 Not practising what you preach

We frequently come across examples of trainees not practising what they preach (we would assume that all health professionals are guilty of this inconsistency on some occasions). If you do not use REBT in your own life, then some of the following problems are likely to occur: REBT has intellectual credibility for you but no emotional conviction, you are unlikely to understand the difficulties that your clients have in translating theory taught in your office into daily real-life experience, you are being inauthentic with your clients and your REBT skills are never honed by 'front line' service, i.e. you are a theoretical REBTer, not an experiential one. In this dialogue, the supervisor wonders when the trainee will start practising REBT:

Supervisor: I made some criticisms of your session tape and you said, the exact words were, 'I'm useless.' What's wrong with your conclusion?

Trainee: I don't understand.

Supervisor: Imagine your client was a counselling trainee who said the same thing as you just did, what would you say to her?

Trainee: Well, I'd encourage her to focus on learning from her errors but without condemning herself as a person for making them. Self-acceptance, in other words.

Supervisor: Exactly. When are you going to start practising REBT on yourself?

Trainee: (sheepishly) I don't know.

Supervisor: What prevents you from practising it on yourself?

Trainee: Well, they're clients, and I'm not.

Supervisor: So, they need REBT, but you don't. You're still fallible and prone to emotional disturbance just like your clients. If you don't practise REBT on yourself, it will stay up here (tapping forehead) and never get into your gut (patting stomach). You'll be a poor role model for REBT.

Trainee: I didn't train in REBT to turn out as a poor role model; so I will start practising REBT on myself.

Supervisor: Good. Remember, it's not just starting practising but continuing it over the long-term.

Key Point

Practise what you preach!

Epilogue

Correcting 101 errors in your REBT practice may seem like a mountain to climb in order to become an accomplished therapist. Scaling this Everest of errors only seems so formidable if you assume you are making *all* the mistakes listed in this book. We do not make this assumption. Focus on correcting those errors you consistently make (e.g. some assessment and disputing errors) and study other errors in the book as a preventive measure (you might be developing bad habits in other areas of REBT). Persist with the steady elimination of errors from your practice but without an accompanying utopian vision of an eventual error-free practice (hardly!). It is important to accept yourself for making the error, then focus on correcting it – putting yourself down only wastes time, holds back your progress and leaves the error intact for longer. We leave you with the eminently wise words of Paul Hauck on dealing with errors:

> You tried something, you found out you were wrong, and now you know what *not* to do next time. Eureka! You have learned something. Isn't that important? Isn't it the product of some daring, some effort, and a drive to learn?
>
> So why do you punish yourself when you have benefited so much? Be glad you have the openness to realize you erred because then you can change. If you were so defensive that you didn't let yourself know you erred, you'd repeat that act endlessly.
>
> Therein is the paradox. No matter how often you make mistakes you are not 'failing'. As long as you are trying (discovering new errors) you are not failing. Failure is doing nothing (1980: 139–40).

References

Beal, D. and DiGiuseppe, R. (1998) 'Training supervisors in rational emotive behavior therapy', Journal of Cognitive Psychotherapy, 12 (2): 127–137.

Bernard, M. E. (1986) Staying Rational in an Irrational World: Albert Ellis and Rational-Emotive Therapy. Carlton, Australia: McCulloch.

Burns, D. D. (1981) Feeling Good: The New Mood Therapy: New York: Signet.

Burns, D. D. (1989) The Feeling Good Handbook. New York: William Morrow.

Cormier, W. H. and Cormier, L. S. (1985) Interviewing Strategies For Helpers, 2nd edition. Monterey, CA: Brooks/Cole.

DiGiuseppe, R. (1991) 'Comprehensive cognitive disputing in RET', in M. E. Bernard (ed.), Using Rational-Emotive Therapy Effectively: A Practitioner's Guide. New York: Plenum.

Dryden, W. (1990) Creativity in Rational-Emotive Therapy. Loughton, Essex: Gale Centre Publications.

Dryden, W. (1994) Progress in Rational Emotive Behaviour Therapy. London: Whurr.

Dryden, W. (1995) Preparing For Client Change in Rational Emotive Behaviour Therapy. London: Whurr.

Dryden, W. (1996) Learning From Demonstration Sessions. London: Whurr.

Dryden, W., Neenan, M. and Yankura, J. (1999) Counselling Individuals: A Rational Emotive Behavioural Handbook, 3rd edition. London: Whurr.

Dryden, W. and Yankura, J. (1995) Developing Rational Emotive Behaviour Therapy. London: Sage.

Ellis, A. (1972) 'Helping people to get better rather than merely feel better', Rational Living, 7 (2): 2–9.

Ellis, A. (1977) 'Fun as psychotherapy', Rational Living, 12 (1): 2–6.

Ellis, A. (1979) 'The issue of force and energy in behavior change', Journal of Contemporary Psychotherapy, 10: 83–97.

Ellis, A. (1983) (pamphlet) The Case Against Religiosity. New York: The Albert Ellis Institute for Rational Emotive Behavior Therapy.

Ellis, A. (1991) 'Using RET effectively: reflections and interview', in M. E. Bernard (ed.), Using Rational-Emotive Therapy Effectively. New York: Plenum.

Ellis, A. (1994) Reason and Emotion in Psychotherapy, revised and updated. New York: Birch Lane Press.

Ellis, A. and Bernard, M. E. (eds.) (1985) Clinical Applications of Rational-Emotive Therapy. New York: Plenum.

Feltham, C. and Dryden, W. (1993) Dictionary of Counselling. London: Whurr.

Fennell, M. J. V. (1989) 'Depression', in K. Hawton, P. M. Salkovskis, J. Kirk, and D. M. Clark (eds.), Cognitive Behaviour Therapy for Psychiatric Problems. Oxford: Oxford University Press.

Grieger, R. and Boyd, J. (1980) Rational-Emotive Therapy: A Skills-Based Approach. New York: Van Nostrand Reinhold.

Hauck, P. A. (1980) Brief Counseling with RET. Philadelphia, PA: Westminster Press.

Moore, R. H. (1988) 'Inference as "A" in rational-emotive therapy', in W. Dryden and P. Trower (eds.), Developments in Rational-Emotive Therapy. Milton Keynes: Open University Press.

Neenan, M. and Dryden, W. (1999) Rational Emotive Behaviour Therapy: Advances in Theory and Practice. London: Whurr.

Neenan, M. and Dryden, W. (2000) Essential Rational Emotive Behaviour Therapy. London: Whurr.

Padesky, C. A. and Greenberger, D. (1995) Clinician's Guide to Mind Over Mood. New York: Guilford.

Persons, J. B. (1989) Cognitive Therapy in Practice: A Case Formulation Approach. New York: Norton.

Rorer, L. G. (1999) 'Dealing with the intellectual-insight problem in cognitive and rational emotive behavior therapy', Journal of Rational-Emotive and Cognitive-Behavior Therapy, 17 (4): 217–236.

Terjesen, M. D., DiGiuseppe, R. and Naidich, J. (1997) 'REBT for anger and hostility', in J. Yankura and W. Dryden (eds.), Using REBT with Common Psychological Problems: A Therapist's Casebook. New York: Springer.

Walen, S. R., DiGiuseppe, R. and Dryden, W. (1992) A Practitioner's Guide to Rational-Emotive Therapy, 2nd edition. New York: Oxford University Press.

Wessler, R. A. and Wessler, R. L. (1980) The Principles and Practice of Rational-Emotive Therapy. San Francisco, CA: Jossey-Bass.

Index